I0016319

Django Full Stack
Development

Learn how to build the building blocks of your website, structure
content, apply stunning styles, and add interactive elements that make
your website feel alive.

Katie Millie

Django Full Stack Development

Learn how to build the building blocks of your website, structure content, apply stunning styles, and add interactive elements that make your website feel alive.

By

Katie Millie

Copyright notice

Copyright © 2024 Katie Millie. All rights Reserved.

All content on this website, including but not limited to
text, graphics, logos, images, audio clips, digital
downloads, and data compilations, is the property of
Katie Millie unless otherwise stated. This content is
protected by international copyright laws.

You are granted a limited license to access and make
personal use of this website. This license does not permit
you to download or modify any portion of it without
express written consent from Katie Millie.

Any unauthorized use, reproduction, or distribution of
the content on this website may result in civil and
criminal penalties.

Katie Millie reserves all rights not expressly granted in
this copyright notice.

Thank you for respecting the intellectual property rights
of Katie Millie. We appreciate your cooperation.

Django Full Stack Development

Table of Contents

Django Full Stack Development

10

INTRODUCTION

Unleash Your Inner Web Alchemist: Mastering Django Full Stack Development

The digital landscape stretches before you, a vast and vibrant canvas yearning for your creative touch. You envision a website – not just any website, but a dynamic, user-friendly masterpiece that captures imaginations and ignites action. But how do you bridge the gap between your brilliant ideas and a live, breathing website? Enter Django, the powerful Python framework that empowers you to become a full-stack web development alchemist, transforming your vision into reality.

This book isn't a dry technical manual; it's your adventure companion, guiding you step-by-step through the exhilarating world of Django full stack development. Forget the intimidation of complex code and jargon-filled tutorials. We'll break down the fundamentals in a way that's clear, engaging, and (dare we say) fun! Here's a glimpse of the empowering journey that awaits:

Unveiling the Magic: The Core Concepts of Django Full Stack

Our adventure begins with a solid foundation. We'll delve into the core concepts of web development, explaining how Django interacts with databases, translates your ideas into stunning web pages, and seamlessly connects the front-end (what users see) with the back-end (the website's engine). Imagine crafting user interfaces that are intuitive and user-friendly, forms that submit flawlessly, and data that flows smoothly behind the scenes. You'll master these skills and more,becoming a true web development sorcerer.

From Pixels to Power: Mastering the Front-End with HTML, CSS, and JavaScript

No website is complete without a captivating facade. We'll equip you with the essential tools to craft the visual magic users experience – HTML, CSS, and JavaScript. Learn how to build the building blocks of your website, structure content, apply stunning styles, and add interactive elements that make your website feel alive. Imagine turning your design ideas into reality, pixel by pixel, and crafting a user experience that is both beautiful and engaging.

Delving into the Depths: Database Mastery with Django's ORM

A website without data is like a story without characters. We'll unlock the power of Django's Object-Relational Mapper (ORM), a powerful tool that allows you to interact with databases seamlessly. Imagine storing and managing user information, blog posts, or product data with ease, giving your website the lifeblood it needs to thrive.

Building the Fortress: Securing Your Website Like a Pro

In today's digital world, security is paramount. We'll delve into the essential security measures needed to safeguard your website from online threats. Learn how to protect user data, prevent hacking attempts, and build trust with your visitors. With your newfound knowledge, you can rest assured your website is a secure fortress, ready to withstand any digital assault.

Deployment Demystified: Witnessing Your Creation Come Alive

The moment of truth is here! We'll guide you through the deployment process, transforming your code into a fully-fledged, live website. Imagine the thrill of witnessing your creation come to life, accessible to the world. From local development environments to cloud deployment options, we'll cover everything you need to launch your website with confidence.

The Art of the Craft: Pro Tips, Troubleshooting, and Real-World Projects

This book goes beyond the basics, equipping you with the knowledge and skills professional developers use. Discover invaluable shortcuts, best practices, and troubleshooting techniques that elevate your development workflow. We'll even guide you through building real-world projects, solidifying your newfound knowledge and preparing you to tackle any web development challenge.

This book is your key to unlocking the full potential of Django full stack development. Are you ready to

embark on this transformative journey? Become a web development alchemist, turn your ideas into reality, and leave your mark on the digital landscape. Scroll up, click "Buy Now," and begin your epic web development adventure!

Chapter 1

Unveiling the Power of Django

Django, a high-level Python web framework, has gained immense popularity for its simplicity, scalability, and robustness in building web applications. With its batteries-included philosophy, Django provides developers with everything they need to create complex, database-driven websites efficiently. In this guide, we'll delve into the core concepts of Django full stack development, exploring its components and demonstrating how to build a complete web application from scratch.

1. Setting Up Django Environment

Before diving into Django development, let's set up our development environment. Ensure you have Python installed on your system, then install Django using pip:

```bash
pip install django
```

Once Django is installed, create a new project:

```bash
django-admin startproject myproject
```

```
```

Navigate into the project directory:

```bash
cd myproject
```

Now, let's create our first Django app:

```bash
python manage.py startapp myapp
```

2. Creating Models

Django's ORM (Object-Relational Mapping) simplifies database management by allowing developers to work with database models as Python objects. Define your models in `models.py` within your app directory. For example:

```python
# myapp/models.py
from django.db import models

class Post(models.Model):
    title = models.CharField(max_length=100)
    content = models.TextField()
```

```python
    created_at =
models.DateTimeField(auto_now_add=True)

    def __str__(self):
        return self.title
```

After defining your models, run migrations to create corresponding database tables:

```bash
python manage.py makemigrations
python manage.py migrate
```

3. Building Views

Views in Django handle user requests and return appropriate responses. Create views in `views.py` within your app directory. For example:

```python
# myapp/views.py
from django.shortcuts import render
from .models import Post

def index(request):
    posts = Post.objects.all()
    return render(request, 'index.html', {'posts': posts})
```

```
```

4. Setting Up URLs

URL routing in Django maps URLs to views. Define
your URL patterns in `urls.py` within your app directory.
For example:

```python
# myapp/urls.py
from django.urls import path
from . import views

urlpatterns = [
    path('', views.index, name='index'),
```

Then, include your app's URLs in the project's `urls.py`:

```python
# myproject/urls.py
from django.contrib import admin
from django.urls import path, include

urlpatterns = [
    path('admin/', admin.site.urls),
    path('', include('myapp.urls')),
]
```

```
```

5. Creating Templates

Templates in Django allow for dynamic HTML
rendering. Create HTML templates within a `templates`
directory inside your app directory. For example, create
`index.html`:

```html
<!-- myapp/templates/index.html -->
<!DOCTYPE html>
<html lang="en">
<head>
    <meta charset="UTF-8">
    <title>My Blog</title>
</head>
<body>
    <h1>Welcome to My Blog</h1>
    <ul>
        {% for post in posts %}
            <li>{{ post.title }}</li>
        {% endfor %}
    </ul>
</body>
</html>
```

6. Running the Development Server

Now, start the Django development server to see your application in action:

```bash
python manage.py runserver
```

Visit `http://127.0.0.1:8000` in your web browser to view your Django app.

7. Adding User Authentication

Django provides built-in support for user authentication. To add authentication to your app, simply enable the authentication middleware and URL patterns in your project's settings:

```python
# myproject/settings.py
INSTALLED_APPS = [
    ...
    'django.contrib.auth',
    'django.contrib.contenttypes',
    'django.contrib.sessions',
    'django.contrib.messages',
    'django.contrib.staticfiles',
```

```
MIDDLEWARE = [

'django.contrib.auth.middleware.AuthenticationMiddlew
are',

'django.contrib.messages.middleware.MessageMiddlewa
re',

'django.contrib.sessions.middleware.SessionMiddleware'
,
```
```

With authentication enabled, you can now protect views
and restrict access to authenticated users only.

## 8. Deploying Django Application

To deploy your Django application to a production
server, you can use various hosting platforms such as
Heroku, AWS, or DigitalOcean. Ensure you follow best
practices for security, scalability, and performance
optimization.

Django's versatility and simplicity make it an ideal
framework for full stack web development. By following
the steps outlined in this guide, you can leverage
Django's powerful features to build robust and scalable
```

web applications efficiently. Experiment with different Django components, explore third-party packages, and continuously refine your skills to unlock the full potential of Django development. Happy coding!

Demystifying Full Stack Development with Django

Full stack development is the art of building web applications that encompass both client-side and server-side components. It involves working with frontend technologies for the user interface and backend technologies for server-side logic and database management. In this guide, we'll demystify full stack development using Django, a powerful Python web framework, to create a complete web application from scratch.

1. Understanding the Full Stack

Full stack development encompasses both frontend and backend development.

- **Frontend**: The frontend is the user-facing part of the application, responsible for presenting data and interacting with users. It typically involves HTML, CSS, and JavaScript, along with frameworks like React, Angular, or Vue.js.

- **Backend**: The backend handles server-side logic, database interactions, and business logic. It consists of languages like Python, Ruby, or Node.js, along with frameworks like Django, Flask, Rails, or Express.js.

2. Django: The Full Stack Framework

Django is a high-level Python web framework that encourages rapid development and clean, pragmatic design. It follows the Model-View-Template (MVT) architecture, which is similar to the Model-View-Controller (MVC) pattern.

- **Models**: Define data models using Django's ORM (Object-Relational Mapping) to interact with the database.

- **Views**: Implement business logic and request handling in views, which render data to templates or return JSON responses.

- **Templates**: Create HTML templates to generate dynamic content and structure the user interface.

3. Setting Up the Project

Let's start by setting up a new Django project:

```bash
django-admin startproject myproject
```

Then, create a new Django app within the project:

```bash
python manage.py startapp myapp
```

4. Building the Backend

- **Models**: Define your data models in `models.py` within your app directory. For example:

```python
# myapp/models.py
from django.db import models

class Post(models.Model):
    title = models.CharField(max_length=100)
    content = models.TextField()
    created_at = models.DateTimeField(auto_now_add=True)

    def __str__(self):
        return self.title
```

```
```

- **Views**: Implement views in `views.py` within your app directory. For example:

```python
# myapp/views.py
from django.shortcuts import render
from .models import Post

def index(request):
    posts = Post.objects.all()
    return render(request, 'index.html', {'posts': posts})
```

5. Creating the Frontend

- **Templates**: Create HTML templates within a `templates` directory inside your app directory. For example:

```html
<!-- myapp/templates/index.html -->
<!DOCTYPE html>
<html lang="en">
<head>
    <meta charset="UTF-8">
    <title>My Blog</title>
```

```
</head>
<body>
    <h1>Welcome to My Blog</h1>
    <ul>
        {% for post in posts %}
            <li>{{ post.title }}</li>
        {% endfor %}
    </ul>
</body>
</html>
```

- **Static Files:** Manage static files like CSS, JavaScript, and images in a `static` directory inside your app directory.

6. URL Routing

Define URL patterns to map URLs to views. Create `urls.py` files within your app directory and project directory to define URL routing.

7. Running the Development Server

Start the Django development server to preview your application:

```bash
```

```
python manage.py runserver
```
```

Visit `http://127.0.0.1:8000` in your web browser to
view your Django app.

## 8. Deploying the Application

To deploy your Django application to a production
server, you can use platforms like Heroku, AWS, or
DigitalOcean. Ensure you follow best practices for
security, scalability, and performance optimization.

Full stack development with Django allows you to create
robust, scalable web applications efficiently. By
combining frontend and backend technologies
seamlessly, you can build dynamic, interactive web
experiences for users. Experiment with different Django
components, explore third-party packages, and
continuously refine your skills to become proficient in
full stack development. Happy coding!

## Why Django? Advantages and Applications

Django, a high-level Python web framework, has
become one of the most popular choices for web
development due to its simplicity, scalability, and
versatility. In this comprehensive guide, we'll explore the
```

advantages of using Django and its various applications, backed by real-world examples and code snippets.

Advantages of Django:

1. Rapid Development: Django follows the "Don't Repeat Yourself" (DRY) principle, enabling developers to build web applications quickly with less code. Its built-in features, such as ORM, admin interface, and authentication system, streamline development.

2. Scalability: Django's architecture allows for horizontal scaling, making it suitable for handling large-scale applications with high traffic. Its modular design and support for caching mechanisms ensure optimal performance as the application grows.

3. Security: Django emphasizes security best practices, including protection against common web vulnerabilities like SQL injection, cross-site scripting (XSS), and cross-site request forgery (CSRF). Its built-in security features help developers mitigate risks and protect user data.

4. Versatility: Django is versatile and can be used to build various types of web applications, including content management systems (CMS), e-commerce platforms, social networks, and APIs. Its flexibility and extensibility make it suitable for a wide range of projects.

5. Community and Ecosystem: Django has a vibrant community of developers who contribute to its ecosystem by creating reusable apps, plugins, and libraries. This vast ecosystem provides developers with a wealth of resources and solutions to common development challenges.

Applications of Django:

1. Content Management Systems (CMS): Django's admin interface makes it an excellent choice for building CMS platforms. Developers can quickly create custom content types, manage user permissions, and perform administrative tasks with ease. Example: Wagtail CMS.

2. E-commerce Platforms: Django's robustness and scalability make it well-suited for building e-commerce websites. Developers can leverage Django's ORM and built-in authentication system to create secure and feature-rich online stores. Example: Saleor.

3. Social Networks: Django's authentication system and user management features make it suitable for building social networking platforms. Developers can implement user profiles, friend connections, and activity feeds using

Django's flexible framework. Example: Django Social Network.

4. API Development: Django can be used to build RESTful APIs for web and mobile applications. Its built-in serialization and authentication capabilities simplify API development, allowing developers to focus on building and delivering scalable APIs. Example: Django REST Framework.

5. Data Analysis Platforms: Django's integration with data analysis libraries like Pandas and NumPy makes it suitable for building data analysis and visualization platforms. Developers can create interactive dashboards and reports using Django's web framework. Example: Django Data Analysis Platform.

Code Example: Building a Simple Blog with Django:

Let's illustrate the advantages and applications of Django by building a simple blog application.

1. Setting Up the Project:

```bash
django-admin startproject myproject
cd myproject
python manage.py startapp blog
```

```
```

2. Defining Models:

```python
# blog/models.py
from django.db import models

class Post(models.Model):
    title = models.CharField(max_length=100)
    content = models.TextField()
    created_at = models.DateTimeField(auto_now_add=True)

    def __str__(self):
        return self.title
```

3. Creating Views:

```python
# blog/views.py
from django.shortcuts import render
from .models import Post

def index(request):
    posts = Post.objects.all()
    return render(request, 'index.html', {'posts': posts})
```

```
```

4. Creating Templates:

```html
<!-- blog/templates/index.html -->
<!DOCTYPE html>
<html lang="en">
<head>
    <meta charset="UTF-8">
    <title>My Blog</title>
</head>
<body>
    <h1>Welcome to My Blog</h1>
    <ul>
        {% for post in posts %}
            <li>{{ post.title }}</li>
        {% endfor %}
    </ul>
</body>
</html>
```

5. Setting Up URLs:

```python
# blog/urls.py
from django.urls import path
```

```python
from . import views

urlpatterns = [
    path('', views.index, name='index'),
]
```

```python
# myproject/urls.py
from django.contrib import admin
from django.urls import path, include

urlpatterns = [
    path('admin/', admin.site.urls),
    path('', include('blog.urls')),
]
```

6. Running the Development Server:

```bash
python manage.py runserver
```

Visit `http://127.0.0.1:8000` in your web browser to view your Django blog.

Django's advantages, including rapid development, scalability, security, versatility, and a vibrant ecosystem, make it a top choice for building a wide range of web applications. Its applications span across content management systems, e-commerce platforms, social networks, API development, and data analysis platforms. By leveraging Django's powerful features and community support, developers can create robust, feature-rich web applications efficiently.

Setting the Stage: Your Development Environment for Django Full Stack Development

Setting up a robust development environment is crucial for efficient Django full stack development. In this guide, we'll walk through the process of setting up your development environment, including installing Python, Django, setting up a virtual environment, and configuring essential tools for coding, version control, and database management.

1. Installing Python

Python is the primary programming language used for Django development. Before getting started, ensure you have Python installed on your system. You can download and install Python from the official website (https://www.python.org/). It's recommended to use the latest stable version of Python.

Once Python is installed, you can verify the installation by opening a terminal or command prompt and typing:

```bash
python --version
```

This command should display the installed Python version.

2. Setting Up a Virtual Environment

A virtual environment isolates your project's dependencies from other projects, ensuring compatibility and preventing conflicts between packages. To create a virtual environment for your Django project, follow these steps:

- Open a terminal or command prompt.

- Navigate to your project directory.

- Run the following command to create a virtual environment named 'venv':

```bash
python -m venv venv
```

Activate the virtual environment:

On Windows:

```bash
venv\Scripts\activate
```

On macOS and Linux:

```bash
source venv/bin/activate
```

Once activated, you'll see '(venv)' prefix in your terminal, indicating that the virtual environment is active.

3. Installing Django

With the virtual environment activated, you can now install Django using pip, Python's package manager:

```bash
```

pip install django
```

This command will install the latest version of Django within your virtual environment.

## 4. Configuring Your IDE

Choosing the right Integrated Development Environment (IDE) can significantly impact your productivity and workflow. Popular IDEs for Django development include PyCharm, Visual Studio Code, and Sublime Text. Configure your IDE according to your preferences, ensuring syntax highlighting, code completion, and debugging tools are enabled for Python and Django development.

## 5. Setting Up Version Control

Version control is essential for tracking changes to your codebase, collaborating with other developers, and managing project history. Git is the most widely used version control system. Follow these steps to set up Git for your Django project:

- Install Git from the official website (https://git-scm.com/).
```

- Open a terminal or command prompt and navigate to your project directory.

- Initialize a Git repository:

```bash
git init
```

Add your project files to the repository:

```bash
git add .
```

Commit the changes:

```bash
git commit -m "Initial commit"
```

Optionally, set up a remote repository on a hosting service like GitHub, GitLab, or Bitbucket, and push your code to the remote repository:

```bash
git remote add origin <remote_repository_url>
git push -u origin master
```

```
```

6. Database Configuration

Django supports multiple databases, including SQLite (default), PostgreSQL, MySQL, and Oracle. Depending on your project requirements, you can configure Django to use the appropriate database backend. To configure a database for your Django project:

a. Open your project's settings.py file.

b. Locate the DATABASES configuration dictionary.

c. Modify the 'ENGINE', 'NAME', 'USER', 'PASSWORD', 'HOST', and 'PORT' settings according to your database configuration.

```python
# settings.py
DATABASES = {
    'default': {
        'ENGINE': 'django.db.backends.sqlite3',
        'NAME': BASE_DIR / 'db.sqlite3',
```

Replace the SQLite configuration with the appropriate settings for your chosen database backend.

7. Running the Development Server

Once your development environment is set up, you can start the Django development server to preview your application locally. Navigate to your project directory in the terminal, activate the virtual environment (if not already activated), and run the following command:

```bash
python manage.py runserver
```

This command will start the development server, and you can access your Django application by visiting `http://127.0.0.1:8000` in your web browser.

Setting up a robust development environment is the first step towards successful Django full stack development. By installing Python, setting up a virtual environment, configuring essential tools like IDE and version control, and configuring the database, you can create a conducive environment for building Django web applications efficiently. With the development server running, you're ready to embark on your Django journey and bring your web development projects to life. Happy coding!

A Glimpse of the Journey Ahead: Book Roadmap for Django Full Stack Development

Embarking on a journey into Django full stack development is an exciting endeavor. To guide you through this adventure, let's outline a roadmap that will help you navigate the various concepts, tools, and techniques involved in building robust web applications with Django.

1. Introduction to Django:

The journey begins with an introduction to Django, where you'll learn about its history, features, and benefits. Dive into the Model-View-Template (MVT) architecture, understand the core components of Django, and explore its ecosystem of tools and libraries.

2. Setting Up Your Development Environment:

Next, we'll focus on setting up your development environment. Learn how to install Python, set up a virtual environment, install Django, configure your IDE, and set up version control with Git. By the end of this stage, you'll have a fully functional environment ready for Django development.

3. Django Fundamentals:

Once your environment is set up, it's time to delve into the fundamentals of Django. Explore the Django project structure, understand how to define models, create views, and build templates. Learn about URL routing, middleware, and settings configuration. By mastering the fundamentals, you'll lay a solid foundation for building Django web applications.

4. Database Management with Django:

Django offers excellent support for database management, with built-in support for various database backends like SQLite, PostgreSQL, MySQL, and Oracle. Learn how to configure your database settings, define database models using Django's ORM (Object-Relational Mapping), perform database migrations, and interact with the database through Django's query API.

5. Building Dynamic Web Pages:

With a solid understanding of Django fundamentals and database management, it's time to start building dynamic web pages. Explore advanced template features, including template inheritance, template tags, and template filters. Learn how to pass data from views to templates, render dynamic content, and handle forms using Django's form handling capabilities.

6. Authentication and Authorization:

Security is paramount in web development, and Django provides robust authentication and authorization mechanisms out of the box. Learn how to implement user authentication, handle user registration and login, manage user sessions, and enforce access control with Django's built-in authorization system. Understand best practices for securing your Django applications against common web vulnerabilities.

7. RESTful API Development with Django:

In today's interconnected world, building APIs is essential for creating scalable and flexible web applications. Learn how to build RESTful APIs with Django REST Framework, a powerful toolkit for building Web APIs in Django. Explore serializers, views, viewsets, authentication, and pagination, and learn how to create APIs that can be consumed by web and mobile clients.

8. Frontend Development with Django:

While Django excels at backend development, integrating frontend technologies is essential for creating modern web applications. Learn how to integrate frontend frameworks like React, Vue.js, or Angular with Django, and explore techniques for building single-page applications (SPAs) and progressive web apps (PWAs). Understand how to manage static files, handle client-side routing, and communicate with the backend through APIs.

9. Deployment and Scaling:

As your Django application grows, deploying it to a production environment becomes crucial. Learn how to deploy Django applications to popular hosting platforms like Heroku, AWS, or DigitalOcean. Understand best practices for configuring production settings, setting up HTTPS, monitoring performance, and scaling your application to handle increased traffic and load.

10. Continuous Learning and Exploration:

Finally, the journey doesn't end here. The world of Django full stack development is vast and ever-evolving. Continue to explore new Django features, experiment with third-party packages, contribute to the Django community, and stay up-to-date with the latest trends and best practices in web development.

By following this roadmap, you'll embark on a rewarding journey into Django full stack development, mastering the tools and techniques needed to build powerful, scalable, and secure web applications. Whether you're a beginner or an experienced developer, the Django ecosystem offers endless opportunities for learning, growth, and innovation. Enjoy the journey ahead!

Chapter 2

The Web Development Trifecta: Front-End, Back-End, and Databases

Django is a high-level Python web framework that encourages rapid development and clean, pragmatic design. It follows the Model-View-Controller (MVC) architectural pattern, though in Django, it's often referred to as Model-View-Template (MVT). Django's primary goal is to ease the creation of complex, database-driven websites. It handles much of the web development "plumbing" so you can focus on writing your app without needing to reinvent the wheel.

- **Front-End Development with Django:** Front-end development in Django typically involves creating templates using Django's template language (DTL), HTML, CSS, and JavaScript. Templates allow you to dynamically generate HTML content based on data from your backend. Let's create a simple template to render a list of items:

```html
<!-- templates/index.html -->
<!DOCTYPE html>
<html lang="en">
```

```
<head>
    <meta charset="UTF-8">
    <meta name="viewport" content="width=device-
width, initial-scale=1.0">
    <title>My Django App</title>
    <link rel="stylesheet" href="{% static 'css/styles.css'
%}">
</head>
<body>
    <h1>Welcome to My Django App!</h1>
    <ul>
        {% for item in items %}
            <li>{{ item }}</li>
        {% endfor %}
    </ul>
    <script src="{% static 'js/scripts.js' %}"></script>
</body>
</html>
```

- **Back-End Development with Django:** Backend development in Django involves defining
  models, views, and URLs. Models represent your
  database tables, views handle HTTP requests,
  and URLs map URLs to view functions. Let's
  create a simple model to represent items in our
  app:

```python
# models.py
from django.db import models

class Item(models.Model):
    name = models.CharField(max_length=100)

    def __str__(self):
        return self.name
```

- **Database Integration with Django:** Django supports various databases, including SQLite (default), PostgreSQL, MySQL, and Oracle. You can define your database settings in the `settings.py` file. Let's configure Django to use a PostgreSQL database:

```python
# settings.py
DATABASES = {
    'default': {
        'ENGINE': 'django.db.backends.postgresql',
        'NAME': 'mydatabase',
        'USER': 'myuser',
        'PASSWORD': 'mypassword',
        'HOST': 'localhost',
        'PORT': '5432',
```

```
        }
    ```
```

- **Migrations**: After defining models, you need to create database tables. Django provides a built-in migration system to manage database schema changes. Run the following commands to create and apply migrations:

```
python manage.py makemigrations
python manage.py migrate
```

- **Integration of Front-End and Back-End:** To integrate the front-end with the back-end, we'll create a view to handle requests and render the template with data from the database.

```python
# views.py
from django.shortcuts import render
from .models import Item

def index(request):
    items = Item.objects.all()
    return render(request, 'index.html', {'items': items})
```
```

- **URL Configuration:** Map the URL to the view function in the `urls.py` file.

```python
# urls.py
from django.urls import path
from . import views

urlpatterns = [
    path('', views.index, name='index'),
]
```

- **Creating a RESTful API:** Django REST Framework (DRF) is a powerful toolkit for building Web APIs. You can create RESTful APIs using DRF in Django. Let's create a simple API to retrieve items.

```python
# api.py
from rest_framework import serializers, viewsets
from .models import Item

class ItemSerializer(serializers.ModelSerializer):
    class Meta:
        model = Item
        fields = '__all__'
```

```python
class ItemViewSet(viewsets.ModelViewSet):
    queryset = Item.objects.all()
    serializer_class = ItemSerializer
```

- **URL Configuration for API:** Map the API URLs to viewsets in the `urls.py` file.

```python
# urls.py
from django.urls import path, include
from rest_framework import routers
from .api import ItemViewSet

router = routers.DefaultRouter()
router.register(r'items', ItemViewSet)

urlpatterns = [
    path('', include(router.urls)),
]
```

In this article, we've explored the Django full-stack development trifecta, covering front-end, back-end, and database integration. Django's powerful features make it a popular choice for building web applications efficiently and securely. With Django, you can create complex web applications with ease, thanks to its extensive documentation, vibrant community, and rich ecosystem of third-party packages. Whether you're a beginner or an experienced developer, Django provides the tools you need to bring your web development ideas to life.

HTTP Requests and Responses: The Language of the Web

HTTP (Hypertext Transfer Protocol) is the foundation of data communication on the World Wide Web. It defines how messages are formatted and transmitted, and how web servers and browsers should respond to various commands. Understanding HTTP is essential for web developers as it governs how data is exchanged between clients and servers.

- **HTTP Requests:** HTTP requests are messages sent by a client (usually a web browser) to request information from a server. There are several types of HTTP requests, but the most common ones are GET, POST, PUT, DELETE, etc. Each request consists of a method, a URL, headers, and optionally, a message body. Let's explore each part using Django:

```python
# views.py
```

```python
from django.http import HttpResponse

def index(request):
    if request.method == 'GET':
        return HttpResponse("This is a GET request.")
    elif request.method == 'POST':
        return HttpResponse("This is a POST request.")
```

In this example, we define a view function that responds differently based on the HTTP method used in the request.

- **HTTP Responses:** HTTP responses are messages sent by a server back to the client in response to an HTTP request. Like requests, responses consist of a status line, headers, and an optional message body. The status line includes the HTTP status code, indicating whether the request was successful, redirected, or encountered an error. Here's how to send different types of responses in Django:

```python
# views.py
from django.http import HttpResponse,
HttpResponseRedirect
```

```python
def index(request):
    if request.method == 'GET':
        return HttpResponse("This is a GET request.")
    elif request.method == 'POST':
        return HttpResponseRedirect('/success')
```

In this example, we send an HTTP response with a status code of 302 (Found) and redirect the client to the '/success' URL.

- **HTTP Headers:** HTTP headers provide additional information about the request or response and can include things like content type, content length, cache control directives, and authentication credentials. Django allows you to set and access headers easily:

```python
# views.py
from django.http import HttpResponse

def index(request):
    response = HttpResponse("This is a response with custom headers.")
    response['Custom-Header'] = 'Value'
    return response
```

In this example, we set a custom header called 'Custom-Header' with the value 'Value' in the HTTP response.

- **Cookies and Sessions:** HTTP cookies are small pieces of data sent from a website and stored on the user's computer by the user's web browser while the user is browsing. Sessions are a way to store information across multiple requests from the same user. Django provides built-in support for cookies and sessions:

```python
# views.py
from django.http import HttpResponse

def index(request):
    response = HttpResponse("This is a response with a cookie.")
    response.set_cookie('cookie_name', 'cookie_value')
    return response
```

In this example, we set a cookie named 'cookie_name' with the value 'cookie_value' in the HTTP response.

- **RESTful APIs and JSON Responses:** RESTful APIs are designed to be stateless and typically

use JSON (JavaScript Object Notation) for data
exchange. Django makes it easy to create
RESTful APIs and send JSON responses:

```python
# views.py
import json
from django.http import JsonResponse

def api(request):
    data = {'message': 'Hello, World!'}
    return JsonResponse(data)
```

In this example, we return a JSON response with the
data {'message': 'Hello, World!'}.

HTTP Requests and Responses are the language of the
web, governing how data is exchanged between clients
and servers. In this article, we've explored the
fundamentals of HTTP, including requests, responses,
headers, cookies, sessions, RESTful APIs, and JSON
responses, in the context of Django full-stack
development. Understanding these concepts is crucial for
building modern web applications efficiently and
securely. With Django, handling HTTP communication
becomes straightforward, allowing developers to focus
on building robust and scalable web solutions.

Understanding Web Servers: The Powerhouse Behind Websites

In the world of web development, the term "web server" is often thrown around, but what exactly is a web server, and why is it crucial for the functioning of websites? In this guide, we'll delve into the intricacies of web servers, focusing specifically on their role in Django full-stack development.

What is a Web Server?

A web server is a software application or hardware device responsible for serving content to users over the internet. When you visit a website, your browser sends a request to the web server hosting that site, and the server responds by delivering the requested content, which could be HTML, CSS, JavaScript, images, videos, or any other type of file.

In the context of Django full-stack development, the web server plays a central role in serving Django applications to users. Django is a high-level Python web framework that encourages rapid development and clean, pragmatic design. It provides developers with a set of tools and features for building web applications, including an ORM (Object-Relational Mapper) for interacting with databases, a URL routing system, a templating engine, and more.

The Django Development Process

Before diving into the specifics of web servers in Django development, let's briefly outline the typical Django development process:

1. Project Setup: Create a new Django project using the `django-admin` command-line tool.

2. App Creation: Within the project, create one or more Django apps to organize your code.

3. Model Definition: Define the data models for your application using Django's ORM.

4. URL Configuration: Map URL patterns to views within your Django apps.

5. View Implementation: Write view functions or classes to handle incoming requests and generate responses.

6. Template Design: Create HTML templates to render dynamic content.

7. Static Files Handling: Serve static files such as CSS, JavaScript, and images.

8. Database Configuration: Configure Django to use a specific database engine (e.g., SQLite, PostgreSQL, MySQL).

9. Development Server: During development, use Django's built-in development server to test your application locally.

10. Deployment: When ready, deploy your Django application to a production server for public access.

At every step of this process, the web server plays a crucial role in serving the application to users and handling their requests.

Django's Built-in Development Server

During the development phase, Django provides a convenient built-in development server that you can use to run your application locally. This server is lightweight and easy to use, making it ideal for testing and debugging purposes. To start the development server, navigate to your project directory and run the following command:

```bash
python manage.py runserver
```

By default, the development server runs on port 8000, but you can specify a different port if needed. Once the server is running, you can access your Django application by visiting `http://localhost:8000` in your web browser.

While the development server is useful for local development, it is not suitable for production use. It lacks important features such as robust performance, security enhancements, and scalability capabilities.

Deploying Django Applications with Production Web Servers

When it comes to deploying Django applications for production use, you'll need to use a production-ready web server. There are several options available, but two of the most popular choices are:

1. Apache: A widely-used open-source web server known for its reliability and versatility. Apache can be configured to serve Django applications using the `mod_wsgi` module, which allows Apache to communicate with Django's WSGI (Web Server Gateway Interface) application interface.

2. Nginx: A high-performance web server and reverse proxy server known for its efficiency and scalability. Nginx can be used to serve Django applications directly or in conjunction with a WSGI server like Gunicorn.

Setting up Django with Gunicorn and Nginx

Let's walk through the process of setting up a Django application with Gunicorn and Nginx on a Linux-based server. This setup is a common choice for deploying Django applications in production environments.

1. Install Dependencies: Install Python, Django, Gunicorn, and Nginx on your server.

2. Configure Gunicorn: Create a Gunicorn configuration file for your Django application. This file specifies the location of your Django project's WSGI application and other settings such as the number of worker processes.

3. Test Gunicorn: Start Gunicorn to ensure that it can serve your Django application correctly. You can do this by running the following command:

```bash
gunicorn --bind 0.0.0.0:8000
myproject.wsgi:application
```

Replace `myproject.wsgi:application` with the path to your project's WSGI application.

4. Configure Nginx: Create a new Nginx server block (virtual host) to proxy requests to Gunicorn. This configuration ensures that Nginx serves static files directly and forwards dynamic requests to Gunicorn.

5. Test Nginx: Restart Nginx and test your Django application to ensure that it is being served correctly through Nginx.

6. Set up Firewall Rules: If necessary, configure your server's firewall to allow traffic on the ports used by Nginx and Gunicorn.

Once you've completed these steps, your Django application should be successfully deployed and accessible to users through Nginx.

Web servers are the powerhouse behind websites, responsible for serving content to users and handling their requests. In Django full-stack development, web servers play a crucial role in serving Django applications to users, both during the development phase and in production environments.

By understanding the role of web servers and how to deploy Django applications with production-ready servers like Apache and Nginx, developers can ensure that their applications are performant, secure, and scalable in real-world scenarios. Whether you're building a small personal website or a large-scale web application, choosing the right web server and deployment strategy is essential for success.

Introduction to Models, Views, and Templates (MVT): Django's Backbone

In the world of web development, especially with Django, understanding the Model-View-Template (MVT) architecture is crucial. MVT is a variation of the Model-View-Controller (MVC) design pattern, and it serves as the backbone of Django's framework. In this guide, we'll explore each component of MVT, how they interact with each other, and their significance in Django full-stack development.

1. Models

Models are the heart of any Django application. They represent the structure and behavior of the data in your application. In Django, models are defined using Python classes that subclass `django.db.models.Model`. Each model class corresponds to a database table, and each attribute of the model represents a database field.

Let's create a simple model to represent a blog post:

```python
# models.py

from django.db import models

class Post(models.Model):
    title = models.CharField(max_length=100)
    content = models.TextField()
    date_posted =
models.DateTimeField(auto_now_add=True)
```

In this example, we've created a `Post` model with three fields: `title`, `content`, and `date_posted`. The `title` field is a character field with a maximum length of 100 characters, the `content` field is a text field for longer content, and the `date_posted` field is a DateTime field that automatically sets the current date and time when a new post is created.

2. Views

Views are responsible for processing user requests and returning responses. In Django, views are Python functions or classes that receive HTTP requests and return HTTP responses. Views interact with models to fetch or manipulate data and with templates to render HTML content.

Let's create a view to display a list of blog posts:

```python
views.py

from django.shortcuts import render
from .models import Post

def post_list(request):
    posts = Post.objects.all()
    return render(request, 'blog/post_list.html', {'posts': posts})
```

In this example, we've defined a view function called `post_list` that retrieves all the posts from the database using the `Post.objects.all()` method and passes them to a template called `post_list.html` as a context variable named `posts`.

3. Templates

Templates are HTML files that define the structure and layout of the user interface. In Django, templates use a built-in template engine called the Django template language (DTL) to generate dynamic content. Templates can contain placeholders and template tags that are replaced with actual data when the template is rendered.

Let's create a template to display the list of blog posts:

```html
<!-- post_list.html -->

<!DOCTYPE html>
<html lang="en">
<head>
    <meta charset="UTF-8">
    <title>Blog Post List</title>
</head>
<body>
    <h1>Blog Posts</h1>
    <ul>
        {% for post in posts %}
            <li>{{ post.title }}</li>
        {% endfor %}
    </ul>
</body>
```

```
</html>
```
` ` `

In this template, we use a `for` loop to iterate over the `posts` context variable passed from the view, and for each post, we display its `title` attribute within an `<li>` element.

How MVT Works Together

Now that we've covered the individual components of MVT, let's see how they work together in a Django application:

1. User Interaction: When a user makes a request to view a list of blog posts, Django's URL routing mechanism maps the request to the appropriate view function (`post_list` in this case).

2. View Processing: The `post_list` view function retrieves the list of posts from the database using the `Post.objects.all()` method.

3. Template Rendering: The view passes the list of posts to the `post_list.html` template as a context variable named `posts`. The template then renders the HTML content dynamically, replacing placeholders with actual data.

4. Response Generation: The rendered HTML content is returned as an HTTP response to the user's browser, where it is displayed as a web page.

5. Model-View Interaction: If the user interacts with the web page (e.g., submits a form to create a new post), the request is again routed to the appropriate view function, which may interact with models to update the database.

Advanced Features and Concepts

While the basic MVT architecture provides a solid foundation for Django development, there are several advanced features and concepts that can enhance the functionality and maintainability of your Django applications:

- **Model Relationships:** Django supports various types of model relationships, such as one-to-many, many-to-one, and many-to-many relationships, which allow you to represent complex data structures and query related objects efficiently.

- **Class-Based Views:** In addition to function-based views, Django also provides class-based views, which offer a more object-oriented approach to view development and can help reduce code duplication and improve code organization.

- **Template Inheritance:** Django templates support inheritance, allowing you to create base templates that define common elements of your site's layout and structure, and then extend or override these templates in child templates to customize their content.

- **Form Handling:** Django provides built-in form handling capabilities, allowing you to create HTML forms easily, validate user input, and process form submissions. Forms can be defined using Django's form classes or generated automatically from model definitions.

The Model-View-Template (MVT) architecture is the backbone of Django's framework, providing a structured approach to building web applications. Models define the data structure, views handle user requests and generate responses, and templates define the presentation layer. By understanding how these components interact with each other, developers can create powerful and maintainable web applications with Django. Whether you're building a simple blog or a complex web application, mastering MVT is essential for success in Django full-stack development.

Exploring Different Website Architectures: A Deep Dive into Options for Django Full-Stack Development

When it comes to building websites with Django, developers have various architectural choices to consider. The architecture of a website defines how its components are organized, how they interact with each other, and how the application logic is divided. In this guide, we'll explore different website architectures in the context of Django full-stack development, along with code examples to illustrate each approach.

1. Monolithic Architecture

Monolithic architecture is one of the simplest and most traditional approaches to building websites. In a monolithic architecture, all the components of the application, including the user interface, business logic, and data access layers, are tightly coupled and deployed as a single unit.

Pros:

- **Simplicity**: Monolithic architectures are straightforward to develop and deploy.

- **Tight Integration:** All components are closely interconnected, making it easy to share data and functionality.

Cons:

- **Scalability Challenges:** Scaling individual components of a monolithic application can be challenging.

- **Maintenance Complexity:** As the application grows, maintaining and updating a monolithic codebase can become difficult.

Let's see how a monolithic Django application might be structured:

```plaintext
myproject/
├── manage.py
├── myapp/
│   ├── migrations/
│   ├── templates/
│   │   └── index.html
│   ├── __init__.py
```

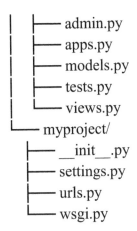

```
|     ├── admin.py
|     ├── apps.py
|     ├── models.py
|     ├── tests.py
|     └── views.py
└── myproject/
      ├── __init__.py
      ├── settings.py
      ├── urls.py
      └── wsgi.py
```

In this example, all components of the application, including models, views, and templates, are organized within a single Django app (`myapp`).

2. Microservices Architecture

Microservices architecture is an alternative approach to building websites, where the application is divided into smaller, independently deployable services, each responsible for a specific aspect of functionality. Each microservice is developed, deployed, and scaled independently, allowing for greater flexibility and scalability.

Pros:

- **Scalability**: Individual microservices can be scaled independently to handle varying levels of traffic.

- **Flexibility**: Each microservice can be developed using different technologies and programming languages, depending on its requirements.

<u>Cons</u>:

- **Complexity**: Managing multiple microservices adds complexity to the development, deployment, and monitoring processes.

- **Communication Overhead:** Inter-service communication can introduce latency and overhead, especially in distributed environments.

Let's see how a microservices architecture might be implemented in Django:

```plaintext
myproject/
    ├── manage.py
    ├── service1/
    │   ├── manage.py
    │   ├── service1/
    │   │   ├── __init__.py
```

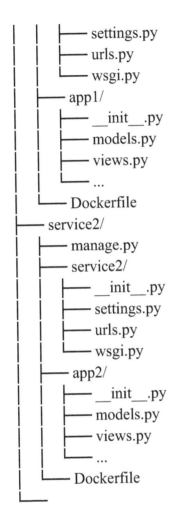

```
│   │   ├── settings.py
│   │   ├── urls.py
│   │   └── wsgi.py
│   ├── app1/
│   │   ├── __init__.py
│   │   ├── models.py
│   │   ├── views.py
│   │   └── ...
│   └── Dockerfile
├── service2/
│   ├── manage.py
│   ├── service2/
│   │   ├── __init__.py
│   │   ├── settings.py
│   │   ├── urls.py
│   │   └── wsgi.py
│   ├── app2/
│   │   ├── __init__.py
│   │   ├── models.py
│   │   ├── views.py
│   │   └── ...
│   └── Dockerfile
└──
```

In this example, each microservice (`service1`, `service2`, etc.) is implemented as a separate Django project, with its own set of models, views, and URLs. Each microservice can be deployed and scaled independently using containers (e.g., Docker) or serverless platforms.

3. Serverless Architecture

Serverless architecture is an emerging trend in web development, where developers focus on writing code without worrying about server management or infrastructure provisioning. In a serverless architecture, applications are built using cloud-based services (e.g., AWS Lambda, Azure Functions) that automatically scale and manage the underlying infrastructure.

Pros:

- **Simplified Operations:** Developers can focus on writing code without managing servers or infrastructure.

- **Scalability**: Serverless platforms automatically scale to handle varying levels of traffic.

Cons:

- **Vendor Lock-in:** Serverless architectures may tie you to a specific cloud provider's ecosystem, limiting flexibility.

- **Cold Start Latency:** Serverless functions may experience cold start latency, especially for infrequently accessed services.

Let's see how a serverless architecture might be implemented with Django:

```plaintext
myproject/
├── manage.py
├── app/
│   ├── __init__.py
│   ├── models.py
│   ├── views.py
│   └── ...
└── serverless_function/
    ├── handler.py
    ├── requirements.txt
    └── serverless.yml
```

In this example, a Django application (`app`) is packaged as a serverless function using a serverless framework (e.g., Serverless Framework, AWS SAM). The `handler.py` file contains the entry point for the serverless function, and the `serverless.yml` file defines the configuration and deployment settings.

There are various website architectures to consider when building Django applications, each with its own set of advantages and trade-offs. The choice of architecture depends on factors such as scalability requirements, development team expertise, and project complexity.

- **Monolithic Architecture:** Simple and straightforward, suitable for small to medium-sized projects with predictable traffic patterns.

- **Microservices Architecture:** Offers greater flexibility and scalability but introduces complexity in managing multiple services.

- **Serverless Architecture:** Focuses on writing code without managing servers, ideal for event-driven and scalable applications.

By understanding the characteristics of each architecture and evaluating their suitability for your project requirements, you can make informed decisions to build robust and scalable Django applications.

Chapter 3

Introduction to the Command Line Interface (CLI) in Django Full Stack Development

The Command Line Interface (CLI) is a powerful tool for developers, allowing them to interact with their development environment, execute commands, and automate tasks efficiently. In the context of Django full-stack development, the CLI plays a vital role in project setup, management, and deployment. In this guide, we'll explore the fundamentals of using the CLI in Django development, along with code examples to illustrate common tasks.

Getting Started with the CLI

To use the CLI effectively in Django development, you'll need to have Python and Django installed on your system. Once installed, you can open a terminal or command prompt to start using the CLI.

Creating a New Django Project

The first step in starting a new Django project is to create a new project directory and navigate into it. Then, you can use the `django-admin` command-line tool to create a new Django project:

```bash
django-admin startproject myproject
```

This command will create a new directory named `myproject` containing the necessary files and directories for a Django project.

Creating a New Django App

After creating a Django project, you can create one or more Django apps within the project. Django apps are modular components that encapsulate specific functionality within the project. To create a new app, navigate into the project directory and run the following command:

```bash
python manage.py startapp myapp
```

Replace `myapp` with the desired name of your app. This command will create a new directory named `myapp` containing the files and directories for the Django app.

Running Development Server

Once you have set up your Django project and created one or more apps, you can start the development server to preview your application locally. Navigate into the project directory and run the following command:

```bash
python manage.py runserver
```

This command will start the Django development server, and you can access your application by visiting `http://localhost:8000` in your web browser.

Common CLI Commands in Django

Now that we've covered the basics of setting up a Django project using the CLI, let's explore some common CLI commands used in Django development:

`python manage.py makemigrations`

This command is used to create database migration files based on changes to your models. Whenever you make changes to your models (e.g., adding new fields or modifying existing ones), you need to generate migration files to apply those changes to the database schema.

```bash
python manage.py makemigrations
```

`python manage.py migrate`

This command applies database migrations to update the database schema based on the migration files created with `makemigrations`.

```bash
python manage.py migrate
```

`python manage.py createsuperuser`

This command creates a superuser account in the Django admin interface, allowing you to access and manage the admin panel of your Django application.

```bash
python manage.py createsuperuser
```

`python manage.py shell`

This command launches the Django shell, an interactive Python shell with access to your Django project's environment. You can use this shell for testing code snippets, debugging, and interacting with your Django models.

```bash
python manage.py shell
```

`python manage.py collectstatic`

This command collects static files from your Django apps and copies them to the `STATIC_ROOT` directory specified in your settings. Static files include CSS, JavaScript, and images used in your application.

```bash
python manage.py collectstatic
```

Custom Management Commands

In addition to built-in management commands provided by Django, you can also create custom management commands to perform specific tasks in your Django project. Custom management commands are defined as

Python functions or classes within the `management/commands` directory of a Django app.

Let's create a custom management command to print a list of all users in the Django application:

```python
# myapp/management/commands/listusers.py

from django.core.management.base import BaseCommand
from django.contrib.auth.models import User

class Command(BaseCommand):
    help = 'Prints a list of all users in the system'

    def handle(self, args, options):
        users = User.objects.all()
        for user in users:

self.stdout.write(self.style.SUCCESS(user.username))
```

To execute this custom management command, you can run the following command:

```bash
python manage.py listusers
```

```
```

The Command Line Interface (CLI) is an essential tool for Django full-stack development, providing developers with a convenient way to interact with their projects, execute commands, and automate tasks. By mastering the CLI and understanding common commands and conventions in Django development, developers can streamline their workflow, improve productivity, and build robust Django applications efficiently. Whether you're setting up a new project, managing database migrations, or creating custom management commands, the CLI is your go-to tool for all things Django.

Navigating the File System with Confidence in Django Full Stack Development

Understanding how to navigate the file system is essential for Django developers, as it allows them to manage project files, organize code, and execute commands efficiently. In this guide, we'll explore various techniques and best practices for navigating the file system in the context of Django full-stack development, accompanied by code examples to illustrate each concept.

Introduction to the File System Structure in Django

Before diving into file navigation techniques, let's first familiarize ourselves with the typical file system structure of a Django project. A Django project typically consists of the following directories and files:

- **Project Directory:** The top-level directory containing the entire Django project.

- **Django Apps:** Individual Django apps, each containing models, views, templates, and other components.

- **Static Files:** Static assets such as CSS, JavaScript, and images used in the project.

- **Templates**: HTML templates used to render dynamic content.

- **Configuration Files:** Files such as `settings.py`, `urls.py`, and `manage.py` that configure and manage the Django project.

Navigating the File System in the Terminal

1. Changing Directories (cd)

The `cd` command is used to change directories in the terminal. You can use it to navigate to different directories within your Django project:

```bash
cd myproject
cd myapp
```

2. Listing Files and Directories (ls)

The `ls` command lists the files and directories in the current directory. You can use it to see what files and directories are present in your Django project:

```bash
ls
ls -l  # Detailed list
```

3. Creating Directories (mkdir)

The `mkdir` command is used to create directories in the file system. You can use it to create new directories for organizing your Django project:

```bash
mkdir new_directory
```

```

```

4. Removing Files and Directories (rm)

The `rm` command is used to remove files and directories from the file system. Be cautious when using this command, as it permanently deletes files and directories:

```bash
rm file.txt
rm -rf directory  # Recursively remove directory and its contents
```

Django Management Commands for File Navigation

In addition to using terminal commands, Django provides built-in management commands to navigate the file system and perform various tasks within a Django project.

1. `startproject`

The `startproject` command is used to create a new Django project. It creates a new directory with the specified project name and initializes the project files:

```bash
django-admin startproject myproject
```

2. `startapp`

The `startapp` command is used to create a new Django app within an existing project. It creates a new directory with the specified app name and initializes the app files:

```bash
python manage.py startapp myapp
```

3. `makemigrations` and `migrate`

The `makemigrations` and `migrate` commands are used to manage database migrations in Django. They generate migration files based on changes to your models and apply those changes to the database schema:

```bash
python manage.py makemigrations
python manage.py migrate
```

4. `collectstatic`

The `collectstatic` command is used to collect static files from Django apps and copy them to a single location for deployment. This command is essential for managing static assets in a Django project:

```bash
python manage.py collectstatic
```

Best Practices for File Navigation in Django

1. Use Meaningful Directory Names: Choose descriptive names for directories and organize files logically within them.

2. Keep File Structure Consistent: Maintain a consistent file structure across your Django projects to make it easier for other developers to understand and navigate the codebase.

3. Use Version Control: Use a version control system like Git to track changes to your project files and collaborate with other developers effectively.

4. Leverage Django Management Commands: Take advantage of Django's built-in management commands to automate common tasks and streamline your workflow.

5. Document Your File Structure: Document the file structure of your Django project, including the purpose of each directory and file, to help new developers onboard more quickly.

Navigating the file system is a fundamental skill for Django developers, allowing them to manage project files, organize code, and execute commands efficiently. By mastering terminal commands and Django management commands, developers can navigate their Django projects with confidence, streamline their workflow, and build robust and maintainable Django applications. Whether you're creating new directories, managing database migrations, or collecting static files, understanding how to navigate the file system effectively is essential for success in Django full-stack development.

Essential Commands for Django Development: Streamlining Your Workflow

In Django full-stack development, mastering essential commands is crucial for efficiently managing projects, running servers, managing databases, and deploying applications. These commands streamline your workflow, automate repetitive tasks, and help you focus on building robust Django applications. In this guide, we'll explore the most essential commands for Django development, accompanied by code examples to illustrate their usage.

1. django-admin startproject

The `startproject` command is used to create a new Django project. It initializes a new project directory with the necessary files and directories to get started with Django development.

```bash
django-admin startproject myproject
```

This command creates a new directory named `myproject` containing the following files:

- `manage.py`: A command-line utility for interacting with the project.

- `myproject/`: The project package containing settings and URL configurations.

- `myproject/settings.py`: Configuration settings for the Django project.

- `myproject/urls.py`: URL routing configuration for the project.

2. python manage.py startapp

The `startapp` command is used to create a new Django app within an existing project. Django apps are modular components that encapsulate specific functionality within the project, such as models, views, and templates.

```bash
python manage.py startapp myapp
```

This command creates a new directory named `myapp` containing the files and directories for the Django app, including:

- `models.py`: Defines data models for the app.

- `views.py`: Contains view functions or classes to handle HTTP requests.

- `urls.py`: Defines URL patterns for the app.

- `templates/`: Directory for HTML templates specific to the app.

3. python manage.py runserver

The `runserver` command starts the Django development server, allowing you to preview your application locally during development.

```bash
python manage.py runserver
```

This command starts the development server on `http://localhost:8000` by default. You can specify a different host and port if needed:

```bash
python manage.py runserver 0.0.0.0:8000
```

4. python manage.py makemigrations and python manage.py migrate

The `makemigrations` command is used to generate database migration files based on changes to your models. It analyzes your models and creates migration files that represent the changes.

```bash
python manage.py makemigrations
```

Once migration files are generated, you can apply them to the database using the `migrate` command:

```bash
python manage.py migrate
```

This command applies pending migrations to synchronize the database schema with your models.

5. python manage.py createsuperuser

The `createsuperuser` command is used to create a superuser account in the Django admin interface. Superusers have access to the admin panel and can manage other users and content in the Django application.

```bash
python manage.py createsuperuser
```

Follow the prompts to enter the desired username, email, and password for the superuser account.

6. python manage.py shell

The `shell` command launches the Django shell, an interactive Python shell with access to your Django project's environment. You can use the shell for testing code snippets, debugging, and interacting with your Django models.

```bash
python manage.py shell
```

7. python manage.py collectstatic

The `collectstatic` command is used to collect static files from Django apps and copy them to a single location for deployment. This command is essential for managing static assets such as CSS, JavaScript, and images in a Django project.

```bash
python manage.py collectstatic
```

8. python manage.py test

The `test` command runs the test suite for your Django project, executing all tests defined in your project's test files. Testing is crucial for ensuring the correctness and reliability of your application.

```bash
python manage.py test
```

Mastering essential commands is essential for efficient
Django development. These commands enable you to
create projects, manage apps, run servers, manage
databases, and deploy applications effectively. By
understanding and using these commands in your
Django workflow, you can streamline your development
process, automate repetitive tasks, and focus on building
robust and scalable Django applications. Whether you're
starting a new project, testing code changes, or
deploying to production, these essential commands are
your go-to tools for Django development success.

Installing and Managing Python Packages for Django Full Stack Development

Python packages play a crucial role in Django full-stack
development, providing developers with pre-built
functionality, tools, and libraries to enhance their
projects. In this guide, we'll explore how to install and
manage Python packages for Django development,
covering common package management tools and best
practices, accompanied by code examples to illustrate
the process.

Introduction to Python Package Management

Python packages are bundles of code, resources, and metadata that extend the functionality of the Python programming language. They can be installed and managed using package management tools such as pip, the Python Package Index (PyPI), and virtual environments. In Django development, Python packages are used to add features, improve performance, and streamline development workflows.

Installing Python Packages with pip

pip is the default package management tool for Python, and it's used to install, upgrade, and uninstall Python packages. You can use pip to install Django and other Python packages required for your Django project.

Installing Django

To install Django, you can use pip with the following command:

```bash
pip install django
```

This command installs the latest version of Django from PyPI (Python Package Index), along with any dependencies required by Django.

Installing Specific Versions

You can also install a specific version of Django by specifying the version number:

```bash
pip install django==3.2.6
```

This command installs Django version 3.2.6 specifically. It's a good practice to specify the version of Django you want to use to ensure compatibility with your project.

Installing Packages from requirements.txt

In Django development, it's common to maintain a `requirements.txt` file listing all the Python packages required for the project. You can use pip to install all the packages listed in the `requirements.txt` file with a single command:

```bash
pip install -r requirements.txt
```

Managing Python Packages with pipenv

pipenv is a higher-level package management tool that simplifies dependency management and virtual environment creation. It combines pip and virtualenv into a single tool and provides additional features such as automatic dependency resolution and lock file generation.

Installing pipenv

You can install pipenv using pip:

```bash
pip install pipenv
```

Creating a Virtual Environment

Once pipenv is installed, you can create a new virtual environment for your Django project:

```bash
pipenv shell
```

This command creates a new virtual environment and activates it. All subsequent pip commands will be executed within this virtual environment.

Installing Django with pipenv

You can install Django and other dependencies for your project using pipenv:

```bash
pipenv install django==3.2.6
```

This command installs Django version 3.2.6 and adds it to the Pipfile, along with its dependencies.

Generating requirements.txt

pipenv automatically generates a `Pipfile` and `Pipfile.lock` to manage project dependencies. You can generate a `requirements.txt` file from the `Pipfile` using the following command:

```bash
pipenv lock --requirements > requirements.txt
```

Using Virtual Environments

Virtual environments are isolated environments that contain specific versions of Python and Python packages. They allow you to install and manage dependencies without affecting the system-wide Python installation. Virtual environments are essential for managing dependencies and ensuring project isolation in Django development.

Creating a Virtual Environment with virtualenv

You can create a virtual environment using virtualenv, a tool for creating isolated Python environments:

```bash
virtualenv venv
```

This command creates a new virtual environment named `venv` in the current directory.

Activating a Virtual Environment

To activate the virtual environment, use the following command:

On Windows:

```bash
venv\Scripts\activate
```

On Unix or MacOS:

```bash
source venv/bin/activate
```

Once activated, the prompt will change to indicate that the virtual environment is active.

Deactivating a Virtual Environment

To deactivate the virtual environment and return to the global Python environment, use the following command:

```bash
deactivate
```

Installing and managing Python packages is essential for Django full-stack development. By using tools like pip, pipenv, and virtual environments, developers can easily install dependencies, manage project dependencies, and ensure project isolation. Whether you're starting a new Django project or working on an existing one, mastering Python package management is key to building robust and scalable Django applications. With the knowledge and techniques outlined in this guide, you'll be well-equipped to handle Python package management in your Django projects effectively.

Version Control with Git: Keeping Track of Your Django Codebase

Version control is a critical aspect of software development, allowing developers to track changes to their codebase, collaborate with team members, and manage project history effectively. Git is the most widely used version control system, and it plays a crucial role in Django full-stack development. In this guide, we'll explore how to use Git for version control in Django projects, covering essential concepts, common workflows, and best practices, accompanied by code examples to illustrate each concept.

Introduction to Git and Version Control

Git is a distributed version control system that tracks changes to files in a project over time. It allows developers to work collaboratively on code, manage project history, and revert to previous states if needed. In Django development, Git is used to track changes to models, views, templates, and other project files, ensuring a smooth and organized development process.

Setting Up Git

Before you can start using Git for version control in your Django project, you need to set up Git on your local machine and configure it with your identity.

Installing Git

You can install Git from the official website (https://git-scm.com/) or using a package manager on your operating system.

Configuring Git

Once Git is installed, you need to configure it with your name and email address:

```bash
git config --global user.name "Your Name"
git config --global user.email "your@email.com"
```

This information will be associated with your commits in the project history.

Initializing a Git Repository

To start using Git for version control in your Django project, you need to initialize a Git repository in the project directory.

```bash
cd myproject
git init
```

This command creates a new Git repository in the `myproject` directory, enabling version control for the project files.

Basic Git Workflow

1. Checking the Status of the Repository

You can use the `git status` command to check the status of the repository and see which files have been modified, staged, or untracked.

```bash
git status
```

2. Adding Files to the Staging Area

Before you can commit changes to the repository, you need to add them to the staging area using the `git add` command.

```bash
git add myapp/models.py
```

This command adds the `models.py` file to the staging area, indicating that it will be included in the next commit.

3. Committing Changes

Once you've added files to the staging area, you can commit them to the repository using the `git commit` command.

```bash
git commit -m "Add new model to the project"
```

This command commits the changes to the repository with a descriptive commit message.

Branching and Merging

Branching and merging are powerful features of Git that allow developers to work on multiple features or fixes simultaneously and merge them back into the main codebase when ready.

Creating a New Branch

You can create a new branch using the `git branch` command and switch to it using `git checkout`.

```bash
git branch new-feature
git checkout new-feature
```

This command creates a new branch named `new-feature` and switches to it.

Merging Branches

Once you've completed work on a branch, you can merge it back into the main codebase using the `git merge` command.

```bash
git checkout main
git merge new-feature
```

This command merges the changes from the `new-feature` branch into the `main` branch.

Collaborating with Remote Repositories

Git allows developers to collaborate with team members by pushing and pulling changes to and from remote repositories hosted on platforms like GitHub, GitLab, or Bitbucket.

Adding a Remote Repository

You can add a remote repository using the `git remote add` command.

```bash
git remote add origin <remote-url>
```

This command adds a remote repository named `origin` with the specified URL.

Pushing Changes

Once you've committed changes to your local repository, you can push them to a remote repository using the `git push` command.

```bash
git push origin main
```

This command pushes the changes from the `main` branch to the `origin` remote repository.

Pulling Changes

To fetch changes from a remote repository and merge them into your local branch, you can use the `git pull` command.

```bash
git pull origin main
```

This command fetches changes from the `main` branch of the `origin` remote repository and merges them into your current branch.

Best Practices for Git Usage in Django Projects

1. Commit Frequently: Make small, atomic commits with descriptive commit messages to track changes effectively.

2. Use Branches: Create branches for new features, bug fixes, and experiments to isolate changes and facilitate collaboration.

3. Review Code Changes: Before committing or merging changes, review the diffs to ensure code quality and correctness.

4. Communicate with Team Members: Coordinate with team members to avoid conflicts and ensure smooth collaboration when working on shared branches.

5. Use `.gitignore`: Exclude unnecessary files and directories from version control by adding them to the `.gitignore` file.

Git is a powerful version control system that plays a crucial role in Django full-stack development. By mastering Git and understanding its fundamental concepts, developers can track changes to their codebase, collaborate with team members, and manage project history effectively. Whether you're working on a new feature, fixing bugs, or collaborating with team members, Git provides the tools and workflows you need to streamline your development process and build robust Django applications. With the knowledge and techniques outlined in this guide, you'll be well-equipped to leverage Git for version control in your Django projects effectively.

Chapter 4

Introduction to HTML Structure and Syntax in Django Full Stack Development

HTML (Hypertext Markup Language) is the standard markup language for creating web pages. It defines the structure and content of a web page using a set of tags and attributes. In Django full-stack development, HTML is used to create templates that render dynamic content generated by Django views. In this guide, we'll explore the basics of HTML structure and syntax, along with code examples to illustrate key concepts in the context of Django development.

Understanding HTML Structure

HTML documents consist of nested elements that define the structure and content of a web page. Each HTML element is enclosed within opening and closing tags, and elements can be nested inside each other to create a hierarchical structure.

Example HTML Document Structure:

```html
<!DOCTYPE html>
```

```html
<html lang="en">
<head>
    <meta charset="UTF-8">
    <meta name="viewport" content="width=device-width, initial-scale=1.0">
    <title>My Django Website</title>
</head>
<body>
    <header>
        <h1>Welcome to My Django Website</h1>
        <nav>
            <ul>
                <li><a href="/">Home</a></li>
                <li><a href="/about/">About</a></li>
                <li><a href="/contact/">Contact</a></li>
            </ul>
        </nav>
    </header>
    <main>
        <section>
            <h2>About Us</h2>
            <p>Lorem ipsum dolor sit amet, consectetur adipiscing elit.</p>
        </section>
    </main>
    <footer>
        <p>&copy; 2024 My Django Website</p>
    </footer>
```

```
</body>
</html>
```
```

## HTML Syntax: Tags and Attributes

### Tags

HTML tags define the structure and content of a web
page. They are enclosed within angle brackets (`< >`)
and typically come in pairs: an opening tag and a closing
tag. Opening tags contain the name of the element, while
closing tags include a forward slash before the element
name. Some tags, like `<img>` and `<br>`, are self-
closing and do not require a closing tag.

Example:
```html
<h1>This is a heading</h1>
<p>This is a paragraph</p>
```
```

Attributes

HTML attributes provide additional information about
an element and are specified within the opening tag.
Attributes consist of a name and a value, separated by an

equals sign (`=`). Common attributes include `class`, `id`, `src`, `href`, `alt`, and `style`.

Example:

```html
<a href="https://www.example.com" class="external-link">Visit Example</a>
<img src="image.jpg" alt="Image Description">
```

Django Templates: Integrating HTML with Django

In Django, HTML templates are used to generate dynamic web pages by combining HTML with Django template syntax. Django templates allow you to insert variables, loops, conditionals, and other logic directly into your HTML code.

Example Django Template Structure:

```html
<!DOCTYPE html>
<html lang="en">
<head>
    <meta charset="UTF-8">
    <meta name="viewport" content="width=device-width, initial-scale=1.0">
```

```
    <title>{{ title }}</title>
  </head>
  <body>
    <header>
      <h1>{{ title }}</h1>
      <nav>
        <ul>
          <li><a href="/">Home</a></li>
          <li><a href="/about/">About</a></li>
          <li><a href="/contact/">Contact</a></li>
        </ul>
      </nav>
    </header>
    <main>
      <section>
        <h2>About Us</h2>
        <p>{{ about_content }}</p>
      </section>
    </main>
    <footer>
      <p>&copy; {{ current_year }} My Django
Website</p>
    </footer>
  </body>
</html>
```

In this Django template, you can see how Django template variables (`{{ title }}`, `{{ about_content }}`, `{{ current_year }}`) are inserted into the HTML code to render dynamic content.

Best Practices for HTML Development in Django

1. Use Semantic HTML: Use semantic HTML elements (e.g., `<header>`, `<nav>`, `<section>`) to improve accessibility and search engine optimization.

2. Separate Structure and Style: Keep HTML structure separate from CSS styles by using external CSS files or inline styles sparingly.

3. Optimize for Accessibility: Ensure your HTML markup is accessible to users with disabilities by following best practices for accessibility.

4. Validate HTML: Use HTML validation tools to check for errors and ensure your HTML code is well-formed and standards-compliant.

5. Test Cross-Browser Compatibility: Test your HTML pages across different web browsers to ensure consistent rendering and functionality.

HTML is a fundamental part of Django full-stack development, used to define the structure and content of web pages. By understanding HTML structure and syntax, along with how to integrate HTML with Django templates, developers can create dynamic and responsive web applications with ease. Whether you're building a simple website or a complex web application, HTML remains the cornerstone of web development in the Django ecosystem. With the knowledge and techniques outlined in this guide, you'll be well-equipped to create compelling and accessible web experiences using HTML in your Django projects.

Creating Headings, Paragraphs, and Lists in Django Full Stack Development

In Django full-stack development, creating structured and well-formatted content is essential for building user-friendly web applications. Headings, paragraphs, and lists are fundamental elements of HTML that help organize and present content effectively. In this guide, we'll explore how to create headings, paragraphs, and lists in Django templates, accompanied by code examples to illustrate each concept.

Headings

Headings are used to define the hierarchy and structure of content on a web page. HTML provides six levels of headings, ranging from `<h1>` for the main heading to `<h6>` for subheadings. Headings should be used to give structure and meaning to the content, making it easier for users to navigate and understand.

Example:

```html
<!DOCTYPE html>
<html lang="en">
<head>
    <meta charset="UTF-8">
    <meta name="viewport" content="width=device-width, initial-scale=1.0">
    <title>My Django Website</title>
</head>
<body>
    <h1>Main Heading</h1>
    <h2>Subheading</h2>
    <h3>Sub-subheading</h3>
    <!-- Additional headings -->
</body>
</html>
```

In Django templates, you can use these HTML heading tags to structure the content of your web pages dynamically.

Paragraphs

Paragraphs are used to display blocks of text or content on a web page. They provide a way to organize and present information in a structured format. In HTML, paragraphs are defined using the `<p>` tag.

Example:

```html
<!DOCTYPE html>
<html lang="en">
<head>
    <meta charset="UTF-8">
    <meta name="viewport" content="width=device-width, initial-scale=1.0">
    <title>My Django Website</title>
</head>
<body>
    <p>This is a paragraph of text.</p>
    <p>This is another paragraph.</p>
</body>
</html>
```

In Django templates, you can use the `<p>` tag to display dynamic text content generated by views or passed as context variables.

Lists

Lists are used to organize and present information in a structured format. HTML provides two types of lists: ordered lists (`<ol>`) and unordered lists (`<ul>`). Ordered lists display items in a numbered sequence, while unordered lists display items with bullet points.

Example:

```html
<!DOCTYPE html>
<html lang="en">
<head>
    <meta charset="UTF-8">
    <meta name="viewport" content="width=device-width, initial-scale=1.0">
    <title>My Django Website</title>
</head>
<body>
    <h2>Ordered List</h2>
    <ol>
        <li>Item 1</li>
```

```
    <li>Item 2</li>
    <li>Item 3</li>
  </ol>

  <h2>Unordered List</h2>
  <ul>
    <li>Item A</li>
    <li>Item B</li>
    <li>Item C</li>
  </ul>
</body>
</html>
```

In Django templates, you can use lists to display dynamic content such as blog posts, product listings, or menu items.

Integrating HTML with Django Templates

In Django full-stack development, HTML is integrated with Django templates to create dynamic web pages. Django templates allow you to insert Python code, variables, loops, and conditionals directly into your HTML code, enabling you to generate dynamic content based on data from views and models.

Example Django Template with Headings, Paragraphs, and Lists:

```html
<!DOCTYPE html>
<html lang="en">
<head>
    <meta charset="UTF-8">
    <meta name="viewport" content="width=device-width, initial-scale=1.0">
    <title>{{ page_title }}</title>
</head>
<body>
    <h1>{{ main_heading }}</h1>

    <h2>Subheading</h2>
    <p>{{ paragraph_content }}</p>

    <h2>List of Items</h2>
    <ul>
        {% for item in item_list %}
        <li>{{ item }}</li>
        {% endfor %}
    </ul>
</body>
</html>
```

In this Django template, you can see how variables (`{{ page_title }}`, `{{ main_heading }}`, `{{ paragraph_content }}`, `{{ item_list }}`) and loops (`{% for item in item_list %}`) are used to dynamically generate HTML content based on data passed from the Django view.

Best Practices for Creating Content in Django Templates

1. Use Semantic HTML: Use HTML elements like headings, paragraphs, and lists appropriately to give structure and meaning to your content.

2. Separate Structure and Style: Keep HTML structure separate from CSS styles by using external CSS files or inline styles sparingly.

3. Use Django Template Tags: Leverage Django template tags and filters to insert dynamic content, perform logic, and format data directly within your HTML code.

4. Optimize for Accessibility: Ensure your HTML markup is accessible to users with disabilities by following best practices for accessibility.

5. Test Across Devices: Test your HTML pages across different devices and screen sizes to ensure a consistent and responsive user experience.

Creating headings, paragraphs, and lists is fundamental in Django full-stack development for organizing and presenting content on web pages. By understanding HTML structure and syntax, along with how to integrate HTML with Django templates, developers can create dynamic and user-friendly web applications. Whether you're building a blog, e-commerce site, or business website, mastering the basics of HTML content creation in Django templates is essential for building successful web applications. With the knowledge and techniques outlined in this guide, you'll be well-equipped to create structured and engaging content in your Django projects.

Linking Between Pages and Embedding Images in Django Full Stack Development

In Django full-stack development, creating a seamless navigation experience between pages and embedding images are essential for building user-friendly web applications. Links allow users to navigate between different sections of a website, while images enhance visual appeal and convey information effectively. In this guide, we'll explore how to create links between pages and embed images in Django templates, accompanied by code examples to illustrate each concept.

Linking Between Pages

Links, also known as hyperlinks, are HTML elements that allow users to navigate between different web pages or sections within the same page. In Django development, links are used to create navigation menus, buttons, and interactive elements that enhance the user experience.

Example:

```html
<!DOCTYPE html>
<html lang="en">
<head>
    <meta charset="UTF-8">
    <meta name="viewport" content="width=device-width, initial-scale=1.0">
    <title>My Django Website</title>
</head>
<body>
    <nav>
        <ul>
            <li><a href="/">Home</a></li>
            <li><a href="/about/">About</a></li>
```

```
        <li><a href="/contact/">Contact</a></li>
    </ul>
    </nav>
</body>
</html>
```

In Django templates, you can use the `<a>` tag to create links to other pages within your website or external URLs.

Dynamic Links in Django Templates

In Django full-stack development, you can create dynamic links in templates to navigate between pages based on data from views and models. Django's template language allows you to insert variables and dynamic content into your HTML code to generate links dynamically.

Example:

```html
<!DOCTYPE html>
<html lang="en">
<head>
    <meta charset="UTF-8">
```

```
    <meta name="viewport" content="width=device-
width, initial-scale=1.0">
    <title>{{ page_title }}</title>
</head>
<body>
    <nav>
        <ul>
            <li><a href="/">Home</a></li>
            <li><a href="/about/">About</a></li>
            <li><a href="/contact/">Contact</a></li>
        </ul>
    </nav>

    <h1>{{ main_heading }}</h1>
    <p>{{ paragraph_content }}</p>
</body>
</html>
```

In this Django template, you can see how variables (`{{ page_title }}`, `{{ main_heading }}`, `{{ paragraph_content }}`) are used to dynamically generate content and links based on data passed from the Django view.

Embedding Images

Images are an essential part of web design, providing visual appeal and conveying information effectively. In Django full-stack development, you can embed images in your web pages using the `<img>` tag.

<u>Example</u>:

```html
<!DOCTYPE html>
<html lang="en">
<head>
    <meta charset="UTF-8">
    <meta name="viewport" content="width=device-width, initial-scale=1.0">
    <title>My Django Website</title>
</head>
<body>
    <h1>Welcome to My Django Website</h1>
    <img src="/static/images/logo.png" alt="Website Logo">
</body>
</html>
```

In Django templates, you can use the `<img>` tag to embed images stored in the `static` directory of your Django project.

Dynamic Image Paths in Django Templates

In Django full-stack development, you can generate dynamic image paths in templates to display images based on data from views and models. This allows you to customize the images displayed on your web pages dynamically.

Example:

```html
<!DOCTYPE html>
<html lang="en">
<head>
    <meta charset="UTF-8">
    <meta name="viewport" content="width=device-width, initial-scale=1.0">
    <title>{{ page_title }}</title>
</head>
<body>
    <h1>{{ main_heading }}</h1>
    <img src="{{ image_path }}" alt="{{ image_alt }}">
</body>
</html>
```

In this Django template, you can see how variables (`{{ page_title }}`, `{{ main_heading }}`, `{{ image_path`

}}`, `{{ image_alt }}`) are used to dynamically generate image paths and alt attributes based on data passed from the Django view.

Best Practices for Linking and Embedding Images in Django

1. Use Descriptive Link Text: Use descriptive link text that accurately describes the destination of the link for better accessibility and user experience.

2. Optimize Image Sizes: Optimize image sizes and formats to improve page load times and user experience, especially on mobile devices.

3. Provide Alt Text: Always provide descriptive alt text for images to improve accessibility and ensure that visually impaired users can understand the content.

4. Organize Image Assets: Organize image assets in the `static` directory of your Django project to keep them separate from other files and facilitate management.

5. Test Cross-Browser Compatibility: Test links and images across different web browsers to ensure consistent rendering and functionality.

Lnking between pages and embedding images are essential aspects of Django full-stack development for creating user-friendly and visually appealing web applications. By understanding how to create links and embed images in Django templates, developers can enhance the navigation experience and visual presentation of their web pages effectively. Whether you're building a simple blog, e-commerce site, or complex web application, mastering the basics of linking and embedding images in Django is essential for building successful web projects. With the knowledge and techniques outlined in this guide, you'll be well-equipped to create dynamic and visually engaging web experiences in your Django projects.

Building Interactive Forms: User Input Made Easy in Django Full Stack Development

Forms play a crucial role in web development, allowing users to submit data and interact with web applications. In Django full-stack development, building interactive forms is essential for creating dynamic and user-friendly web applications. In this guide, we'll explore how to create and handle forms in Django, covering form creation, validation, submission, and processing, accompanied by code examples to illustrate each concept.

Introduction to Forms in Django

Forms in Django are created using Django's form handling framework, which provides a powerful and flexible way to define and process HTML forms. Django forms allow developers to define form fields, validate user input, handle form submission, and process form data seamlessly.

Example Form in Django:

```python
forms.py

from django import forms

class ContactForm(forms.Form):
    name = forms.CharField(label='Your Name',
max_length=100)
    email = forms.EmailField(label='Your Email')
    message = forms.CharField(label='Your Message',
widget=forms.Textarea)
```

In this example, we define a `ContactForm` class with three form fields: `name`, `email`, and `message`.

Creating Form Templates

Once the form is defined in Django, you need to create a template to render the form in HTML and handle user input.

Example Form Template:

```html
<!-- contact_form.html -->

<!DOCTYPE html>
<html lang="en">
<head>
    <meta charset="UTF-8">
    <meta name="viewport" content="width=device-width, initial-scale=1.0">
    <title>Contact Form</title>
</head>
<body>
    <h1>Contact Us</h1>
    <form method="post">
        {% csrf_token %}
        {{ form.as_p }}
        <button type="submit">Submit</button>
    </form>
</body>
</html>
```

In this template, we use the `form` variable to render the form fields (``{{ form.as_p }}``) and include a CSRF token for security (``{% csrf_token %}``).

Handling Form Submission

When a user submits the form, Django processes the form data and invokes the appropriate view function to handle the submission.

Example View Function:

```python
views.py

from django.shortcuts import render
from .forms import ContactForm

def contact(request):
    if request.method == 'POST':
        form = ContactForm(request.POST)
        if form.is_valid():
            # Process form data
            name = form.cleaned_data['name']
            email = form.cleaned_data['email']
            message = form.cleaned_data['message']
            # Additional processing logic
```

```
else:
    form = ContactForm()
return render(request, 'contact_form.html', {'form':
form})
```

In this view function, we check if the request method is
POST, indicating a form submission. We validate the
form using `form.is_valid()` and access the cleaned form
data using `form.cleaned_data`.

Form Validation in Django

Django provides built-in form validation mechanisms to
ensure that user input is accurate and meets the specified
criteria.

Example Form Validation:

```python
forms.py

from django import forms

class ContactForm(forms.Form):
    name = forms.CharField(label='Your Name',
max_length=100)
    email = forms.EmailField(label='Your Email')
```

```
    message = forms.CharField(label='Your Message',
widget=forms.Textarea)

    def clean_message(self):
        message = self.cleaned_data['message']
        if len(message) < 10:
            raise forms.ValidationError("Message must be at
least 10 characters long.")
        return message
```

In this example, we define a `clean_message()` method
to validate the `message` field and raise a
`ValidationError` if the message is too short.

Customizing Form Presentation

Django forms provide flexibility for customizing form
presentation and behavior using widgets, labels, and CSS
classes.

Example Customization:

```python
forms.py

from django import forms
```

```python
class ContactForm(forms.Form):
    name = forms.CharField(label='Your Name',
max_length=100, widget=forms.TextInput(attrs={'class':
'form-control'}))
    email = forms.EmailField(label='Your Email',
widget=forms.EmailInput(attrs={'class': 'form-control'}))
    message = forms.CharField(label='Your Message',
widget=forms.Textarea(attrs={'class': 'form-control'}))
```
```

In this example, we customize the appearance of form fields by adding CSS classes to the form widgets.

## Best Practices for Building Interactive Forms in Django

**1. Use Django Forms:** Leverage Django's built-in form handling framework to streamline form creation, validation, and processing.

**2. Validate User Input:** Implement form validation to ensure that user input is accurate, complete, and meets specified criteria.

**3. Handle Form Submission:** Create view functions to handle form submission, process form data, and perform additional logic as needed.
```

4. Customize Form Presentation: Customize form appearance and behavior using widgets, labels, and CSS classes to enhance user experience.

5. Test Form Functionality: Test forms thoroughly to ensure that they work as expected across different devices, browsers, and user scenarios, including both valid and invalid input.

6. Implement CSRF Protection: Include CSRF tokens in your forms to protect against Cross-Site Request Forgery (CSRF) attacks and ensure the security of form submissions.

7. Use Form Helpers: Take advantage of Django's form helpers, such as form fields, widgets, and validators, to simplify form creation and enhance functionality.

8. Handle Form Errors Gracefully: Display helpful error messages to users when form validation fails, guiding them on how to correct their input and resubmit the form.

Building interactive forms in Django full-stack development is essential for creating dynamic and user-friendly web applications. By leveraging Django's form handling framework, developers can streamline form creation, validation, submission, and processing, providing users with a seamless experience for submitting data and interacting with web applications. Whether you're building a simple contact form, a complex data entry form, or an interactive user registration form, mastering the basics of building interactive forms in Django is crucial for building successful web projects. With the knowledge and techniques outlined in this guide, you'll be well-equipped to create robust and user-friendly forms in your Django applications, enhancing the overall user experience and usability of your web applications.

Structuring Your Website with Semantic HTML in Django Full Stack Development

Semantic HTML provides a way to structure web pages in a meaningful and descriptive manner, enhancing accessibility, search engine optimization (SEO), and maintainability. In Django full-stack development, using semantic HTML is essential for creating well-organized and easy-to-understand web applications. In this guide, we'll explore the importance of semantic HTML and how to structure your website using semantic elements, accompanied by code examples to illustrate each concept.

Importance of Semantic HTML

Semantic HTML refers to using HTML elements that convey meaning about the content they contain. By using semantic elements such as `<header>`, `<nav>`, `<main>`, `<section>`, `<article>`, and `<footer>`, you provide clear structure and context to your web pages, making them more accessible to both users and search engines. Semantic HTML also improves code readability and maintainability by clearly delineating different sections of a web page.

Structuring Your Website with Semantic HTML

1. Header:

The `<header>` element typically contains the introductory content of a web page, including the site's branding, navigation links, and search functionality.

```html
<!DOCTYPE html>
<html lang="en">
<head>
    <meta charset="UTF-8">
    <meta name="viewport" content="width=device-width, initial-scale=1.0">
    <title>My Django Website</title>
</head>
<body>
```

```
    <header>
        <h1>My Django Website</h1>
        <nav>
            <ul>
                <li><a href="/">Home</a></li>
                <li><a href="/about/">About</a></li>
                <li><a href="/contact/">Contact</a></li>
            </ul>
        </nav>
    </header>
</body>
</html>
```

2. Navigation:

The `<nav>` element is used to define navigation links within a web page, providing users with a way to navigate to different sections or pages of the website.

```html
<nav>
    <ul>
        <li><a href="/">Home</a></li>
        <li><a href="/about/">About</a></li>
        <li><a href="/contact/">Contact</a></li>
    </ul>
</nav>
```

```
```

3. Main Content:

The `<main>` element represents the main content area of a web page, containing the primary content that users are interested in.

```html
<main>
  <section>
    <h2>About Us</h2>
    <p>Lorem ipsum dolor sit amet, consectetur adipiscing elit.</p>
  </section>
  <section>
    <h2>Services</h2>
    <p>Lorem ipsum dolor sit amet, consectetur adipiscing elit.</p>
  </section>
</main>
```

4. Section and Article:

The `<section>` element is used to define sections within a web page, while the `<article>` element represents a self-contained piece of content that can be distributed and reused independently.

```html
<section>
    <h2>Services</h2>
    <article>
        <h3>Service 1</h3>
        <p>Lorem ipsum dolor sit amet, consectetur adipiscing elit.</p>
    </article>
    <article>
        <h3>Service 2</h3>
        <p>Lorem ipsum dolor sit amet, consectetur adipiscing elit.</p>
    </article>
</section>
```

5. Footer:

The `<footer>` element typically contains information about the website, such as copyright notices, contact information, and links to privacy policies or terms of service.

```html
<footer>
```

```
    <p>&copy; 2024 My Django Website</p>
</footer>
```

Integrating Semantic HTML with Django Templates

In Django full-stack development, you can integrate
semantic HTML elements with Django templates to
create dynamic and structured web pages.

```html
<!DOCTYPE html>
<html lang="en">
<head>
  <meta charset="UTF-8">
  <meta name="viewport" content="width=device-width, initial-scale=1.0">
  <title>{{ page_title }}</title>
</head>
<body>
  <header>
    <h1>{{ site_name }}</h1>
    <nav>
      <ul>
        <li><a href="/">Home</a></li>
        <li><a href="/about/">About</a></li>
        <li><a href="/contact/">Contact</a></li>
      </ul>
```

```html
    </nav>
  </header>

  <main>
    <section>
      <h2>About Us</h2>
      <p>{{ about_content }}</p>
    </section>
    <section>
      <h2>Services</h2>
      <article>
        <h3>Service 1</h3>
        <p>Lorem ipsum dolor sit amet, consectetur
adipiscing elit.</p>
      </article>
      <article>
        <h3>Service 2</h3>
        <p>Lorem ipsum dolor sit amet, consectetur
adipiscing elit.</p>
      </article>
    </section>
  </main>

  <footer>
    <p>&copy; {{ current_year }} My Django
Website</p>
  </footer>
</body>
```

```
</html>
```
```

In this Django template, we've integrated semantic
HTML elements with Django template variables to
create a dynamic and structured web page.

## Best Practices for Using Semantic HTML in Django

**1. Choose Appropriate Elements:** Select the most
appropriate semantic HTML elements to convey the
structure and meaning of your content effectively.

**2. Keep It Simple:** Use semantic HTML elements
sparingly and avoid overcomplicating your markup with
unnecessary elements.

**3. Ensure Accessibility:** Test your website for
accessibility using tools like screen readers to ensure that
users with disabilities can navigate and understand your
content.

**4. Optimize for SEO:** Semantic HTML can improve
your website's search engine rankings by providing
search engines with clear and meaningful information
about your content.
```

5. Stay Consistent: Maintain consistency in your use of semantic HTML elements throughout your website to provide a cohesive and intuitive user experience.

Structuring your website with semantic HTML is crucial for creating well-organized, accessible, and SEO-friendly web applications in Django full-stack development. By using semantic HTML elements such as `<header>`, `<nav>`, `<main>`, `<section>`, `<article>`, and `<footer>`, you can convey the structure and meaning of your content clearly to both users and search engines. With the knowledge and techniques outlined in this guide, you'll be well-equipped to leverage semantic HTML effectively in your Django projects, resulting in more intuitive and user-friendly web applications.

Chapter 5

Introduction to Cascading Style Sheets (CSS) in Django Full Stack Development

Cascading Style Sheets (CSS) is a stylesheet language used to describe the presentation of a document written in HTML or XML. In Django full stack development, CSS plays a vital role in styling web pages, making them visually appealing, responsive, and user-friendly. In this guide, we'll explore the basics of CSS, including selectors, properties, values, and best practices for integrating CSS with Django templates, accompanied by code examples to illustrate each concept.

Understanding CSS Basics

CSS consists of rulesets that define how HTML elements should be displayed in a web browser. A CSS ruleset consists of a selector, followed by a set of declarations enclosed in curly braces `{}`.

Example CSS Ruleset:

```css
/ Selector /
h1 {
```

```
/ Declarations /
color: blue;
font-size: 24px;
```

In this example, the selector `h1` targets all `<h1>`
elements in the HTML document, and the declarations
within the curly braces specify that the text color should
be blue and the font size should be 24 pixels.

CSS Selectors

CSS selectors are patterns used to select the elements
you want to style. There are various types of CSS
selectors, including element selectors, class selectors, ID
selectors, attribute selectors, and pseudo-selectors.

Example CSS Selectors:

```css
/ Element Selector /
h1 {
    / Styles /
}

/ Class Selector /
.button {
    / Styles /
```

```
}

/ ID Selector /
#navbar {
   / Styles /
}

/ Attribute Selector /
input[type="text"] {
   / Styles /
}

/ Pseudo-class Selector /
a:hover {
   / Styles /
}
```

CSS Properties and Values

CSS properties define the visual appearance of HTML elements, while values specify the specific characteristics of those properties.

Example CSS Properties and Values:

```css
/ Property: color /
```

```
h1 {
   color: blue; / Value: blue /
}

/ Property: font-size /
h1 {
   font-size: 24px; / Value: 24 pixels /
}

/ Property: background-color /
.button {
   background-color: #ff0000; / Value: red /
}

/ Property: margin /
.container {
   margin: 20px; / Value: 20 pixels /
}
```
```

## Integrating CSS with Django Templates

In Django full-stack development, CSS can be integrated
with Django templates to style HTML elements
dynamically and create visually appealing web pages.

## Example Django Template with Inline CSS:
```

```html
<!DOCTYPE html>
<html lang="en">
<head>
    <meta charset="UTF-8">
    <meta name="viewport" content="width=device-width, initial-scale=1.0">
    <title>My Django Website</title>
    <style>
      / Inline CSS /
      h1 {
          color: blue;
          font-size: 24px;
      }
      .button {
          background-color: #ff0000;
          color: white;
          padding: 10px 20px;
          border: none;
          border-radius: 5px;
          cursor: pointer;
      }
    </style>
</head>
<body>
    <h1>Welcome to My Django Website</h1>
    <button class="button">Click Me</button>
</body>
```

```
</html>
```
```

```

Best Practices for CSS in Django

1. Use External Stylesheets: Separate CSS styles from HTML content by using external stylesheet files, promoting code maintainability and reusability.

2. Organize CSS Code: Organize CSS code logically and consistently to facilitate readability and ease of maintenance.

3. Use Selectors Wisely: Choose appropriate CSS selectors to target specific elements and avoid overusing generic selectors, which can lead to unintended styling conflicts.

4. Optimize for Performance: Minify and concatenate CSS files to reduce file size and improve page load times, enhancing overall performance.

5. Test Across Browsers: Test CSS styles across different web browsers and devices to ensure consistent rendering and compatibility.

Cascading Style Sheets (CSS) is a powerful tool in Django full-stack development for styling web pages and creating visually appealing user interfaces. By understanding CSS basics, including selectors, properties, and values, and integrating CSS with Django templates, developers can enhance the presentation and usability of their web applications. With the knowledge and best practices outlined in this guide, you'll be well-equipped to leverage CSS effectively in your Django projects, creating engaging and user-friendly web experiences for your users.

Styling Text, Backgrounds, and Borders in Django Full Stack Development

In Django full-stack development, styling text, backgrounds, and borders using Cascading Style Sheets (CSS) is essential for creating visually appealing and engaging web applications. With CSS, you can customize the appearance of text, set background colors or images, and define borders around elements to enhance the overall design and user experience. In this guide, we'll explore various CSS properties and techniques for styling text, backgrounds, and borders, accompanied by code examples to illustrate each concept within the context of Django templates.

Styling Text

CSS provides a wide range of properties to style text, including font properties, text color, text alignment, text decoration, and text shadow.

Example CSS for Styling Text:

```css
/ Font Family /
body {
    font-family: Arial, sans-serif;
}

/ Font Size /
h1 {
    font-size: 24px;
}

/ Font Weight /
strong {
    font-weight: bold;
}

/ Text Color /
p {
    color: #333333;
}

/ Text Alignment /
```

```css
.text-center {
    text-align: center;
}

/ Text Decoration /
a {
    text-decoration: none;
}

/ Text Shadow /
h2 {
    text-shadow: 2px 2px 4px rgba(0, 0, 0, 0.5);
}
```

Styling Backgrounds

You can use CSS to style backgrounds by setting
background colors, images, gradients, and positions.

Example CSS for Styling Backgrounds:

```css
/ Background Color /
.header {
    background-color: #f2f2f2;
}
```

```
/ Background Image /
.hero-section {
    background-image: url('hero-image.jpg');
    background-size: cover;
    background-position: center;
}

/ Background Gradient /
.gradient-background {
    background: linear-gradient(to right, #ff7e5f,
#feb47b);
}

/ Background Position /
.footer {
    background-image: url('footer-pattern.png');
    background-repeat: repeat-x;
    background-position: bottom;
}
```
`` `

Styling Borders

CSS allows you to create borders around elements using properties like border width, border color, border style, and border radius.

Example CSS for Styling Borders:

```css
/ Border Width /
.box {
  border-width: 2px;
}

/ Border Color /
.card {
  border-color: #cccccc;
}

/ Border Style /
.button {
  border-style: solid;
}

/ Border Radius /
.rounded-border {
  border-radius: 5px;
}
```

Integrating CSS with Django Templates

You can integrate CSS styles with Django templates by
either using inline CSS, embedded CSS in `<style>` tags

within the HTML document, or by linking external CSS files.

<u>Example Django Template with Embedded CSS:</u>

```html
```html
<!DOCTYPE html>
<html lang="en">
<head>
  <meta charset="UTF-8">
  <meta name="viewport" content="width=device-width, initial-scale=1.0">
  <title>Styling Text, Backgrounds, and Borders</title>
  <style>
    body {
        font-family: Arial, sans-serif;
        color: #333333;
    }
    .container {
        background-color: #f2f2f2;
        padding: 20px;
    }
    .header {
        text-align: center;
        font-size: 24px;
        margin-bottom: 20px;
    }
    .text-center {
```
```

```css
        text-align: center;
      }
      .box {
        border: 2px solid #cccccc;
        border-radius: 5px;
        padding: 10px;
        margin-bottom: 20px;
      }
      .button {
        background-color: #ff7e5f;
        color: white;
        border: none;
        border-radius: 5px;
        padding: 10px 20px;
        text-align: center;
        display: inline-block;
        text-decoration: none;
      }
      .button:hover {
        background-color: #ff6347;
      }
    </style>
  </head>
  <body>
    <div class="container">
      <h1 class="header">Styling Text, Backgrounds,
and Borders</h1>
      <div class="box">
```

```
    <p>This is a paragraph of styled text.</p>
    <a href="#" class="button">Click Me</a>
  </div>
  <div class="box text-center">
    <p>This is another paragraph of styled text.</p>
    <a href="#" class="button">Click Me</a>
  </div>
 </div>
</body>
</html>
```

Best Practices for Styling Text, Backgrounds, and Borders in Django

1. Consistency: Maintain consistent styling throughout your website to create a cohesive user experience.

2. Accessibility: Ensure text is legible and background colors or images do not hinder readability.

3. Responsiveness: Use responsive design techniques to ensure that text, backgrounds, and borders adapt well to different screen sizes and devices.

4. Performance: Optimize background images and gradients to minimize page load times and improve performance.

5. Browser Compatibility: Test CSS styles across different web browsers to ensure consistent rendering and compatibility.

Styling text, backgrounds, and borders using CSS is essential for creating visually appealing and user-friendly web applications in Django full-stack development. By leveraging CSS properties and techniques, developers can customize the appearance of text, set background colors or images, and define borders around elements to enhance the overall design and user experience. With the knowledge and best practices outlined in this guide, you'll be well-equipped to integrate CSS effectively with Django templates, creating engaging and visually appealing web applications.

Mastering Layout with Display Properties in Django Full Stack Development

In Django full-stack development, mastering layout with CSS display properties is crucial for creating well-structured and visually appealing web applications. CSS display properties allow you to control how elements are rendered and positioned within the layout of a web page. In this guide, we'll explore various CSS display properties, including block, inline, inline-block, flex, and grid, and demonstrate how to use them to create flexible and responsive layouts in Django templates.

Understanding CSS Display Properties

CSS display properties determine how elements are displayed and positioned within the document flow. The most common display values include:

- `block`: Elements with a block display value start on a new line and expand to fill the available horizontal space.

- `inline`: Elements with an inline display value do not start on a new line and only take up as much width as necessary.

- `inline-block`: Elements with an inline-block display value behave like inline elements but can have block-level properties applied to them.

- `flex`: Elements with a flex display value become flex containers, allowing you to control the layout and alignment of their child elements along a flexible axis.

- `grid`: Elements with a grid display value become grid containers, enabling you to create complex two-dimensional layouts with rows and columns.

Using Block and Inline Display

Example CSS for Block and Inline Display:

```css
/ Block Display /
.block-element {
    display: block;
    width: 100%;
    background-color: #f2f2f2;
    padding: 10px;
    margin-bottom: 20px;
}

/ Inline Display /
.inline-element {
    display: inline;
    background-color: #ff0000;
    color: #ffffff;
    padding: 5px 10px;
}
```

Example Django Template with Block and Inline Display:

```html
<!DOCTYPE html>
<html lang="en">
<head>
    <meta charset="UTF-8">
    <meta name="viewport" content="width=device-width, initial-scale=1.0">
    <title>Block and Inline Display</title>
    <style>
      / CSS Styles /
      .block-element {
          display: block;
          width: 100%;
          background-color: #f2f2f2;
          padding: 10px;
          margin-bottom: 20px;
      }

      .inline-element {
          display: inline;
          background-color: #ff0000;
          color: #ffffff;
          padding: 5px 10px;
      }
    </style>
</head>
<body>
```

```
    <div class="block-element">Block Element 1</div>
    <div class="block-element">Block Element 2</div>
    <span class="inline-element">Inline Element
1</span>
    <span class="inline-element">Inline Element
2</span>
</body>
</html>
```

Using Inline-Block Display

Example CSS for Inline-Block Display:

```css
/ Inline-Block Display /
.inline-block-element {
    display: inline-block;
    width: 30%;
    background-color: #cccccc;
    padding: 10px;
    margin-right: 10px;
}
```

Example Django Template with Inline-Block Display:

```html
```

```html
<!DOCTYPE html>
<html lang="en">
<head>
  <meta charset="UTF-8">
  <meta name="viewport" content="width=device-width, initial-scale=1.0">
  <title>Inline-Block Display</title>
  <style>
    / CSS Styles /
    .inline-block-element {
      display: inline-block;
      width: 30%;
      background-color: #cccccc;
      padding: 10px;
      margin-right: 10px;
    }
  </style>
</head>
<body>
  <div class="inline-block-element">Inline-Block Element 1</div>
  <div class="inline-block-element">Inline-Block Element 2</div>
  <div class="inline-block-element">Inline-Block Element 3</div>
</body>
</html>
```
```
```

Using Flexbox Display

Flexbox is a powerful layout model that allows you to create flexible and responsive layouts with ease.

Example CSS for Flexbox Display:

```css
/ Flex Display /
.flex-container {
  display: flex;
  justify-content: space-between;
}

.flex-item {
  flex: 1;
  background-color: #ff6347;
  color: #ffffff;
  padding: 10px;
  margin-right: 10px;
}
```

Example Django Template with Flexbox Display:

```html
<!DOCTYPE html>
```

```html
<html lang="en">
<head>
  <meta charset="UTF-8">
  <meta name="viewport" content="width=device-
width, initial-scale=1.0">
  <title>Flexbox Display</title>
  <style>
    / CSS Styles /
    .flex-container {
      display: flex;
      justify-content: space-between;
    }

    .flex-item {
      flex: 1;
      background-color: #ff6347;
      color: #ffffff;
      padding: 10px;
      margin-right: 10px;
    }
  </style>
</head>
<body>
  <div class="flex-container">
    <div class="flex-item">Flex Item 1</div>
    <div class="flex-item">Flex Item 2</div>
    <div class="flex-item">Flex Item 3</div>
  </div>
```

```
</body>
</html>
```

Using CSS Grid Display

CSS Grid Layout is a two-dimensional layout system that allows you to create complex grid-based layouts.

Example CSS for Grid Display:

```css
/ Grid Display /
.grid-container {
    display: grid;
    grid-template-columns: repeat(3, 1fr);
    grid-gap: 10px;
}

.grid-item {
    background-color: #6cb2eb;
    color: #ffffff;
    padding: 10px;
}
```

Example Django Template with Grid Display:

```html
<!DOCTYPE html>
<html lang="en">
<head>
  <meta charset="UTF-8">
  <meta name="viewport" content="width=device-width, initial-scale=1.0">
  <title>Grid Display</title>
  <style>
    / CSS Styles /
    .grid-container {
      display: grid;
      grid-template-columns: repeat(3, 1fr);
      grid-gap: 10px;
    }
    .grid-item {
      background-color: #6cb2eb;
      color: #ffffff;
      padding: 10px;
    }
  </style>
</head>
<body>
  <div class="grid-container">
    <div class="grid-item">Grid Item 1</div>
    <div class="grid-item">Grid Item 2</div>
    <div class="grid-item">Grid Item 3</div>
  </div>
```

```
</body>
</html>
```
```

## Best Practices for Layout with CSS Display Properties in Django

**1. Consistency:** Maintain consistency in your layout design across different pages and components of your Django application to provide a seamless user experience.

**2. Responsive Design:** Use CSS display properties to create responsive layouts that adapt well to various screen sizes and devices, ensuring usability on both desktop and mobile devices.

**3. Modularization:** Break down your layout into smaller, reusable components and use CSS display properties to arrange them flexibly within the page layout, promoting code maintainability and reusability.

**4. Browser Compatibility:** Test your layout designs across different web browsers to ensure consistent rendering and compatibility, especially when using advanced layout techniques like Flexbox and CSS Grid.
```

5. Performance Optimization: Optimize your layout stylesheets for performance by minimizing the use of complex selectors and reducing redundant CSS rules, improving page load times and overall performance.

Mastering layout with CSS display properties is essential for creating flexible, responsive, and visually appealing web layouts in Django full-stack development. By understanding the various display values, such as block, inline, inline-block, flex, and grid, and how to use them effectively, developers can create sophisticated and dynamic layouts that enhance the user experience of their Django applications. With the knowledge and best practices outlined in this guide, you'll be well-equipped to leverage CSS display properties to create elegant and functional layouts in your Django projects, delivering compelling web experiences to your users.

Responsive Design: Making Your Website Mobile-Friendly in Django Full Stack Development

In today's digital landscape, having a mobile-friendly website is essential for providing a seamless user experience across different devices. Responsive design ensures that your website adapts and looks great on various screen sizes, from desktop computers to smartphones and tablets. In this guide, we'll explore the principles of responsive design and demonstrate how to implement it in Django full-stack development using CSS media queries, flexible layouts, and other techniques.

Understanding Responsive Design

Responsive design is an approach to web design that aims to create websites that automatically adjust their layout and content based on the screen size and device orientation. The goal is to provide an optimal viewing experience for users, regardless of the device they're using to access the website. Key principles of responsive design include:

1. Flexible Grid Layouts: Using relative units like percentages and ems to define layout dimensions, allowing elements to adapt fluidly to different screen sizes.

2. Media Queries: CSS media queries enable you to apply different styles based on the characteristics of the user's device, such as screen width, height, and orientation.

3. Viewport Meta Tag: The viewport meta tag in HTML allows you to control the viewport's size and scale on mobile devices, ensuring proper rendering and responsiveness.

Implementing Responsive Design in Django

1. Using Flexible Units for Layout

```css
/ Example CSS for Flexible Layout /
.container {
    width: 100%;
    max-width: 1200px;
    margin: 0 auto;
    padding: 0 20px;
}

.column {
    width: 100%;
    padding: 0 20px;
    box-sizing: border-box;
}

@media (min-width: 768px) {
    .column {
        width: 50%;
        float: left;
    }
}
```

2. Applying Media Queries

```css
/ Example CSS for Media Queries /
@media (max-width: 768px) {
  .column {
    width: 100%;
    float: none;
```

3. Using the Viewport Meta Tag

```html
<!DOCTYPE html>
<html lang="en">
<head>
  <meta charset="UTF-8">
  <meta name="viewport" content="width=device-width, initial-scale=1.0">
  <title>Responsive Design</title>
  <link rel="stylesheet" href="styles.css">
</head>
<body>
  <!-- Content goes here -->
</body>
</html>
```

Best Practices for Responsive Design in Django

1. Start with Mobile-First: Begin by designing and developing for mobile devices first, then progressively enhance the layout and features for larger screens using media queries.

2. Test Across Devices: Regularly test your website on various devices and screen sizes to ensure consistent rendering and usability across different platforms.

3. Optimize Images: Use responsive images and techniques like srcset and sizes to serve appropriately sized images based on the user's device and viewport size, reducing page load times on mobile devices.

4. Prioritize Content: Prioritize essential content and features for mobile users, ensuring that critical information is accessible and prominently displayed on smaller screens.

5. Accessibility: Ensure that your responsive design is accessible to users with disabilities by following best practices for web accessibility, such as providing text alternatives for images and using semantic HTML markup.

Implementing responsive design in Django full-stack development is crucial for creating mobile-friendly websites that provide an optimal user experience across various devices and screen sizes. By following the principles of flexible layouts, media queries, and viewport meta tags, developers can ensure that their websites adapt seamlessly to the needs of mobile users while maintaining usability and accessibility standards. With the knowledge and techniques outlined in this guide, you'll be well-equipped to create responsive and user-friendly web applications in Django, delivering a consistent experience to users regardless of the device they're using.

Advanced CSS Techniques: Animations and Transitions in Django Full Stack Development

CSS animations and transitions add dynamic and interactive elements to web pages, enhancing the user experience and providing visual feedback. In this guide, we'll explore advanced CSS techniques for creating animations and transitions in Django full-stack development, using keyframe animations, transitions, and practical examples to demonstrate their implementation.

Understanding CSS Animations and Transitions

- **CSS Animations:** CSS animations allow you to create motion effects by defining keyframes that specify the style changes at various points in time. Keyframe animations provide precise control over the animation timeline, allowing you to create complex and dynamic effects.

- **CSS Transitions:** CSS transitions enable smooth and gradual changes in an element's style properties over a specified duration. Transitions are triggered by changes in the element's state, such as hover or click events, and provide a subtle and polished user experience.

Implementing CSS Animations and Transitions in Django

1. Using Keyframe Animations

```css
/ Example CSS for Keyframe Animation /
@keyframes slideIn {
    0% { opacity: 0; transform: translateY(-100%); }
    100% { opacity: 1; transform: translateY(0); }
}
.slide-in {
    animation: slideIn 1s ease-in-out;
```

```
}
```

2. Applying Transitions

```css
/ Example CSS for Transitions /
.button {
    background-color: #3498db;
    color: #ffffff;
    padding: 10px 20px;
    border-radius: 5px;
    transition: background-color 0.3s ease;
}
.button:hover {
    background-color: #2980b9;
}
```

3. Integrating with Django Templates

```html
<!DOCTYPE html>
<html lang="en">
<head>
    <meta charset="UTF-8">
    <meta name="viewport" content="width=device-width, initial-scale=1.0">
```

```
<title>Advanced CSS Techniques</title>
<link rel="stylesheet" href="styles.css">
</head>
<body>
  <div class="container">
    <div class="box slide-in">Animated Box</div>
    <button class="button">Hover Me</button>
  </div>
</body>
</html>
```

Best Practices for CSS Animations and Transitions in Django

1. Performance Optimization: Keep animations and transitions lightweight and optimized for performance to ensure smooth rendering and minimize page load times.

2. Browser Compatibility: Test animations and transitions across different web browsers and devices to ensure consistent behavior and rendering.

3. Accessibility: Ensure that animations and transitions do not hinder accessibility, and provide alternative methods for users with disabilities to interact with dynamic content.

4. Progressive Enhancement: Use feature detection and progressive enhancement techniques to provide fallbacks for browsers that do not support CSS animations and transitions.

5. Consistency: Maintain consistency in animation styles and timing throughout your Django application to provide a cohesive user experience.

CSS animations and transitions are powerful tools for adding interactivity and visual interest to web pages in Django full-stack development. By understanding the principles of keyframe animations and transitions and how to implement them effectively, developers can create engaging and dynamic user experiences that enhance the overall quality of their Django applications. With the knowledge and techniques outlined in this guide, you'll be well-equipped to leverage advanced CSS techniques to create stunning animations and transitions in your Django projects, delighting users and improving usability.

Chapter 6

Understanding the Core Concepts of JavaScript in Django Full Stack Development

JavaScript is a versatile programming language widely used for creating interactive and dynamic web applications. In Django full-stack development, JavaScript plays a crucial role in enhancing user experience, handling client-side interactions, and communicating with backend servers asynchronously. In this guide, we'll explore the core concepts of JavaScript, including variables, data types, functions, control flow, and object-oriented programming, accompanied by code examples to illustrate each concept within the context of Django applications.

Variables and Data Types

Variables in JavaScript are containers for storing data values. JavaScript supports various data types, including numbers, strings, booleans, arrays, and objects.

Example JavaScript Variables and Data Types:

```javascript
// Number
```

```javascript
let age = 30;

// String
let name = "John Doe";

// Boolean
let isStudent = true;

// Array
let fruits = ["apple", "banana", "orange"];

// Object
let person = { name: "John", age: 30 };
```

Functions

Functions in JavaScript are reusable blocks of code that perform a specific task. They can be declared using the `function` keyword or as arrow functions.

Example JavaScript Functions:

```javascript
// Function Declaration
function greet(name) {
    return "Hello, " + name + "!";
}
```

```javascript
// Function Expression
let square = function(num) {
    return num * num;
};

// Arrow Function
let multiply = (a, b) => {
    return a * b;
};
```

Control Flow

JavaScript provides control flow statements such as `if...else`, `switch`, `for`, `while`, and `do...while` to control the execution of code based on conditions.

Example JavaScript Control Flow:

```javascript
// if...else Statement
let num = 10;
if (num > 0) {
    console.log("Positive number");
} else if (num < 0) {
    console.log("Negative number");
} else {
```

```javascript
    console.log("Zero");
}
// Switch Statement
let day = "Monday";
switch (day) {
    case "Monday":
        console.log("Today is Monday");
        break;
    case "Tuesday":
        console.log("Today is Tuesday");
        break;
    default:
        console.log("Unknown day");
        break;
}
// for Loop
for (let i = 0; i < 5; i++) {
    console.log(i);
}

// while Loop
let counter = 0;
while (counter < 5) {
    console.log(counter);
    counter++;
}
```

Object-Oriented Programming (OOP)

JavaScript supports object-oriented programming concepts such as classes, objects, inheritance, and encapsulation.

Example JavaScript OOP:

```javascript
// Class Declaration
class Person {
  constructor(name, age) {
    this.name = name;
    this.age = age;
  }

  greet() {
    console.log("Hello, my name is " + this.name);
  }
}

// Object Instantiation
let john = new Person("John", 30);
john.greet();
```

Integrating JavaScript with Django Templates

You can integrate JavaScript code directly into Django templates using `<script>` tags or by linking external JavaScript files.

Example Django Template with Inline JavaScript:

```html
<!DOCTYPE html>
<html lang="en">
<head>
  <meta charset="UTF-8">
  <meta name="viewport" content="width=device-width, initial-scale=1.0">
  <title>JavaScript in Django</title>
</head>
<body>
  <h1>Hello, Django!</h1>

  <!-- Inline JavaScript -->
  <script>
    let num = 10;
    if (num > 0) {
      console.log("Positive number");
    } else if (num < 0) {
      console.log("Negative number");
    } else {
      console.log("Zero");
    }
```

```
    </script>
  </body>
</html>
```
```

## Best Practices for JavaScript in Django

**1. Modularization:** Organize JavaScript code into separate modules and files to improve code maintainability and reusability.

**2. Error Handling:** Implement error handling mechanisms to gracefully handle runtime errors and exceptions in JavaScript code.

**3. Asynchronous Programming:** Utilize asynchronous programming techniques such as promises and async/await to handle asynchronous tasks like fetching data from backend servers in Django applications.

**4. Optimization:** Optimize JavaScript code for performance by minimizing code size, reducing DOM manipulation, and implementing caching strategies where applicable.

**5. Browser Compatibility:** Test JavaScript code across different web browsers and devices to ensure consistent behavior and compatibility.
```

Understanding the core concepts of JavaScript is essential for developing dynamic and interactive web applications in Django full-stack development. By mastering variables, data types, functions, control flow, and object-oriented programming in JavaScript, developers can create robust client-side functionality and enhance user experience in Django applications. With the knowledge and best practices outlined in this guide, you'll be well-equipped to leverage JavaScript effectively in your Django projects, creating compelling and engaging web applications that meet the needs of modern users.

Manipulating the DOM: Changing Your Website on the Fly in Django Full Stack Development

In Django full-stack development, manipulating the Document Object Model (DOM) using JavaScript is a powerful technique for dynamically updating web pages without reloading the entire page. The DOM represents the structure of an HTML document as a hierarchical tree of objects, and JavaScript allows developers to access, modify, and manipulate these elements in real-time. In this guide, we'll explore how to manipulate the DOM in Django applications, including techniques for adding, removing, and modifying HTML elements dynamically, accompanied by code examples to illustrate each concept.

Understanding the DOM

The DOM is a programming interface for web documents that defines the logical structure of documents and the way a document is accessed and manipulated. Each HTML element in a document is represented as a node in the DOM tree, and JavaScript provides methods and properties for interacting with these nodes.

Accessing DOM Elements

JavaScript provides several methods for accessing DOM elements, including `getElementById()`, `getElementsByClassName()`, `getElementsByTagName()`, and `querySelector()`.

Example JavaScript for Accessing DOM Elements:

```javascript
// Accessing Element by ID
let header = document.getElementById("header");

// Accessing Elements by Class Name
```

```javascript
let paragraphs =
document.getElementsByClassName("paragraph");

// Accessing Elements by Tag Name
let buttons =
document.getElementsByTagName("button");

// Accessing Element by CSS Selector
let container = document.querySelector(".container");
```

Modifying DOM Elements

Once you've accessed DOM elements, you can modify their properties, attributes, and content using JavaScript.

Example JavaScript for Modifying DOM Elements:

```javascript
// Changing Text Content
header.textContent = "New Header Text";

// Changing HTML Content
container.innerHTML = "<p>New content added
dynamically</p>";

// Modifying Attributes
button.setAttribute("disabled", true);
```

```javascript
// Adding CSS Classes
paragraph.classList.add("highlight");

// Removing CSS Classes
container.classList.remove("container");
```

Adding and Removing DOM Elements

JavaScript allows you to dynamically add and remove elements from the DOM tree, enabling dynamic content generation and manipulation.

Example JavaScript for Adding and Removing DOM Elements:

```javascript
// Creating New Element
let newParagraph = document.createElement("p");
newParagraph.textContent = "New paragraph added dynamically";
container.appendChild(newParagraph);

// Removing Element
container.removeChild(newParagraph);
```

Event Handling

JavaScript event handling allows you to respond to user interactions such as clicks, keypresses, and mouse movements, enabling interactive and responsive web applications.

Example JavaScript for Event Handling:

```javascript
// Adding Event Listener
button.addEventListener("click", function() {
    console.log("Button clicked");
});

// Removing Event Listener
button.removeEventListener("click",
eventHandlerFunction);
```

Integrating with Django Templates

You can integrate JavaScript for DOM manipulation directly into Django templates using `<script>` tags or by linking external JavaScript files.

Example Django Template with Inline JavaScript:

```html
```html
<!DOCTYPE html>
<html lang="en">
<head>
    <meta charset="UTF-8">
    <meta name="viewport" content="width=device-
width, initial-scale=1.0">
    <title>DOM Manipulation in Django</title>
</head>
<body>
    <h1 id="header">Header</h1>
    <div class="container">
        <p class="paragraph">Paragraph</p>
        <button id="button">Click Me</button>
    </div>

    <script>
        // JavaScript for DOM Manipulation
        let header = document.getElementById("header");
        header.textContent = "New Header Text";

        let button = document.getElementById("button");
        button.addEventListener("click", function() {
            console.log("Button clicked");
        });
    </script>
</body>
</html>
```
```

```

```

Best Practices for DOM Manipulation in Django

1. Separation of Concerns: Keep JavaScript code separate from HTML markup and CSS styles for better maintainability and readability.

2. Performance Optimization: Minimize DOM manipulation operations and use efficient algorithms to improve performance, especially for large and complex web pages.

3. Cross-Browser Compatibility: Test DOM manipulation code across different web browsers to ensure consistent behavior and compatibility.

4. Progressive Enhancement: Implement graceful degradation and progressive enhancement techniques to ensure that essential functionality remains accessible even without JavaScript enabled.

5.Accessibility: Ensure that dynamically generated content and interactive elements are accessible to users with disabilities by following accessibility best practices and standards.

Manipulating the DOM using JavaScript is a fundamental technique for creating dynamic and interactive web applications in Django full-stack development. By accessing, modifying, adding, and removing DOM elements dynamically, developers can create engaging user experiences and enhance the functionality of their Django applications. With the knowledge and techniques outlined in this guide, you'll be well-equipped to leverage DOM manipulation effectively in your Django projects, creating dynamic and responsive web pages that meet the needs of modern users.

Event Handling: Responding to User Interactions in Django Full Stack Development

Event handling in web development allows developers to respond to various user interactions such as clicks, key presses, mouse movements, and form submissions. In Django full-stack development, JavaScript plays a crucial role in handling these events and providing dynamic and interactive user experiences. In this guide, we'll explore event handling in Django applications, including event types, event listeners, event propagation, and practical examples to demonstrate their implementation.

Understanding Events in JavaScript

Events in JavaScript are actions or occurrences that happen in the browser, triggered by user interactions or system events. Common types of events include:

- **Mouse Events:** Clicks, double-clicks, mouse movements, hover, etc.

- **Keyboard Events:** Key presses, key releases, etc.

- **Form Events:** Submit, focus, blur, etc.

- **Window Events:** Load, resize, scroll, etc.

Event Listeners

Event listeners are functions that listen for specific events and execute a callback function when the event occurs. They allow developers to define custom behavior in response to user interactions.

Example JavaScript Event Listener:

```javascript
// Adding Event Listener to Button Click
let button = document.getElementById("myButton");
```

```
button.addEventListener("click", function() {
    console.log("Button clicked!");
});
```

Event Propagation

Event propagation refers to the process by which events are propagated or "bubbled" up from the target element to its ancestors or "captured" down from the ancestors to the target element. Understanding event propagation is essential for handling events effectively, especially in complex DOM structures.

Example JavaScript Event Propagation:

```html
<!DOCTYPE html>
<html lang="en">
<head>
    <meta charset="UTF-8">
    <meta name="viewport" content="width=device-width, initial-scale=1.0">
    <title>Event Propagation</title>
</head>
<body>
    <div id="outer">
        <div id="inner">
```

```
            <button id="myButton">Click Me</button>
        </div>
    </div>

    <script>
        // Adding Event Listeners to Outer and Inner Divs
        let outerDiv = document.getElementById("outer");
        let innerDiv = document.getElementById("inner");
        let button =
document.getElementById("myButton");

        outerDiv.addEventListener("click", function() {
            console.log("Outer div clicked!");
        });

        innerDiv.addEventListener("click", function() {
            console.log("Inner div clicked!");
        });

        button.addEventListener("click", function(event) {
            event.stopPropagation();
            console.log("Button clicked!");
        });
    </script>
</body>
</html>
```

Integrating Event Handling in Django Templates

You can integrate event handling JavaScript code directly into Django templates using `<script>` tags or by linking external JavaScript files.

Example Django Template with Event Handling:

```html
<!DOCTYPE html>
<html lang="en">
<head>
    <meta charset="UTF-8">
    <meta name="viewport" content="width=device-width, initial-scale=1.0">
    <title>Event Handling in Django</title>
</head>
<body>
    <button id="myButton">Click Me</button>

    <script>
        // Adding Event Listener to Button Click
        let button =
document.getElementById("myButton");
        button.addEventListener("click", function() {
            console.log("Button clicked!");
        });
    </script>
```

```
</body>
</html>
```

Best Practices for Event Handling in Django

1. Delegated Event Handling: Use event delegation to handle events efficiently, especially for dynamically generated or large numbers of elements.

2. Separation of Concerns: Keep event handling logic separate from HTML markup and CSS styles for better maintainability and readability.

3. Error Handling: Implement error handling mechanisms to gracefully handle unexpected errors and exceptions in event handling code.

4. Performance Optimization: Optimize event handling code for performance by minimizing unnecessary event listeners and reducing DOM manipulation operations.

5. Accessibility: Ensure that event-driven interactions are accessible to users with disabilities by providing alternative methods for accessing essential functionality.

Event handling is a fundamental aspect of creating dynamic and interactive web applications in Django full-stack development. By understanding event types, event listeners, event propagation, and best practices for event handling, developers can create engaging user experiences and enhance the functionality of their Django applications. With the knowledge and techniques outlined in this guide, you'll be well-equipped to leverage event handling effectively in your Django projects, providing users with responsive and intuitive interfaces that meet their needs and expectations.

Working with AJAX: Fetching Data Without Page Reloads in Django Full Stack Development

Asynchronous JavaScript and XML (AJAX) is a technique used in web development to fetch data from a server and update parts of a web page without requiring a full page reload. In Django full-stack development, AJAX is commonly used to create dynamic and interactive user experiences, such as updating content, submitting form data, and handling user interactions asynchronously. In this guide, we'll explore how to work with AJAX in Django applications, including sending AJAX requests, handling server responses, and updating the DOM dynamically, with practical examples to illustrate each concept.

Understanding AJAX

AJAX enables web pages to make asynchronous HTTP requests to the server and update specific parts of the page without reloading the entire document. This technique allows for smoother and more responsive user interactions, as only the necessary data is fetched and rendered, reducing page load times and improving the overall user experience.

Sending AJAX Requests

In JavaScript, you can use the `XMLHttpRequest` object or the newer `fetch` API to send AJAX requests to the server. These requests can be of different types, such as GET, POST, PUT, DELETE, etc., depending on the desired action.

Example JavaScript AJAX Request with `fetch` API:

```javascript
fetch('/api/data')
  .then(response => response.json())
  .then(data => {
    console.log(data);
  })
  .catch(error => {
    console.error('Error:', error);
  });
```

```

```

Handling AJAX Responses

Once the server processes the AJAX request, it sends back a response, which can be in various formats such as JSON, XML, HTML, or plain text. In JavaScript, you can handle these responses and update the DOM accordingly.

Example JavaScript Handling AJAX Response:

```javascript
fetch('/api/data')
   .then(response => response.json())
   .then(data => {
     // Update DOM with fetched data
     document.getElementById('content').innerHTML =
data.content;
   })
   .catch(error => {
     console.error('Error:', error);
   });
```

Integrating AJAX with Django

In Django applications, you can create views that handle AJAX requests and return JSON or other data formats as responses. These views can then be accessed via AJAX from your front-end JavaScript code.

Example Django View Handling AJAX Request:

```python
from django.http import JsonResponse

def get_data(request):
    data = {
        'content': 'Dynamic content fetched via AJAX'
    }
    return JsonResponse(data)
```

Best Practices for Working with AJAX in Django

1. CSRF Protection: When making POST requests via AJAX, ensure that CSRF protection is enabled in your Django application to prevent cross-site request forgery attacks.

2. Error Handling: Implement error handling mechanisms to gracefully handle AJAX request failures and server errors in your JavaScript code.

3. Security: Validate and sanitize user input on the server side to prevent security vulnerabilities such as SQL injection and cross-site scripting (XSS) attacks.

4. Performance Optimization: Optimize AJAX requests by minimizing payload size, caching responses where applicable, and leveraging browser caching mechanisms.

5. Progressive Enhancement: Provide fallbacks for users with JavaScript disabled to ensure accessibility and usability of your Django application.

Working with AJAX in Django full-stack development allows developers to create dynamic and interactive web applications that provide a seamless user experience. By sending asynchronous requests to the server, handling responses, and updating the DOM dynamically, developers can create modern web applications that meet the needs of users and deliver content efficiently. With the knowledge and techniques outlined in this guide, you'll be well-equipped to leverage AJAX effectively in your Django projects, enhancing the interactivity and responsiveness of your web applications.

Introduction to JavaScript Frameworks in Django Full Stack Development

JavaScript frameworks have revolutionized web development by providing powerful tools and libraries for building dynamic, responsive, and interactive web applications. In Django full-stack development, JavaScript frameworks play a crucial role in enhancing the front-end user experience, managing client-side data, and simplifying the development process. In this guide, we'll introduce some popular JavaScript frameworks, including React, Vue.js, and Angular, and discuss how they can be integrated into Django applications, with code examples to illustrate their usage.

What are JavaScript Frameworks?

JavaScript frameworks are collections of pre-written JavaScript code designed to simplify the development of web applications by providing reusable components, utilities, and abstractions for common tasks. These frameworks abstract away many of the complexities of web development, allowing developers to focus on building functionality rather than writing boilerplate code.

Popular JavaScript Frameworks

1. React

React is a JavaScript library for building user interfaces, developed by Facebook. It's known for its component-based architecture and virtual DOM, which enable developers to create interactive and reusable UI components. React's declarative syntax and one-way data flow make it easy to build complex UIs and manage state effectively.

Example React Component:

```jsx
import React from 'react';

class MyComponent extends React.Component {
  render() {
    return (
      <div>
        <h1>Hello, React!</h1>
        <p>This is a React component.</p>
      </div>
    }
}
export default MyComponent;
```

2. Vue.js

Vue.js is a progressive JavaScript framework for building user interfaces, designed to be incrementally adoptable. It features a simple and flexible API, reactive data binding, and a component-based architecture similar to React. Vue's gentle learning curve and extensive ecosystem make it a popular choice for developers of all skill levels.

Example Vue Component:

```html
<template>
  <div>
    <h1>Hello, Vue!</h1>
    <p>This is a Vue component.</p>
  </div>
</template>

<script>
export default {
  name: 'MyComponent'
}
</script>
```

3. Angular

Angular is a platform and framework for building single-page client applications using HTML and TypeScript. Developed and maintained by Google, Angular provides a comprehensive set of tools and features for building scalable and maintainable web applications. It follows the MVC (Model-View-Controller) architecture and offers features like dependency injection, routing, and form handling out of the box.

Example Angular Component:

```typescript
import { Component } from '@angular/core';

@Component({
  selector: 'app-my-component',
  template: `
   <div>
     <h1>Hello, Angular!</h1>
     <p>This is an Angular component.</p>
   </div>
})
export class MyComponent {}
```

Integrating JavaScript Frameworks with Django

To integrate JavaScript frameworks like React, Vue.js, and Angular with Django applications, you can use Django's templating engine to render the initial HTML page, and then use the framework's client-side capabilities to handle dynamic updates and interactions.

Example Django Template with React Integration:

```html
<!DOCTYPE html>
<html lang="en">
<head>
  <meta charset="UTF-8">
  <meta name="viewport" content="width=device-width, initial-scale=1.0">
  <title>React Integration with Django</title>
</head>
<body>
  <div id="root"></div>
  <script src="/static/js/main.js"></script>
</body>
</html>
```

Example Django Template with Vue.js Integration:

```html
<!DOCTYPE html>
<html lang="en">
<head>
  <meta charset="UTF-8">
```

```html
    <meta name="viewport" content="width=device-
width, initial-scale=1.0">
    <title>Vue.js Integration with Django</title>
</head>
<body>
    <div id="app">
        <my-component></my-component>
    </div>
    <script src="/static/js/app.js"></script>
</body>
</html>
```

Example Django Template with Angular Integration:

```html
<!DOCTYPE html>
<html lang="en">
<head>
    <meta charset="UTF-8">
    <meta name="viewport" content="width=device-
width, initial-scale=1.0">
    <title>Angular Integration with Django</title>
</head>
<body>
    <app-my-component></app-my-component>
    <script src="/static/js/main.js"></script>
</body>
```

```
</html>
```
```


## Best Practices for Using JavaScript Frameworks in Django

**1. Separation of Concerns:** Keep the front-end and back-end code separate to maintain a clean and modular codebase.

**2. Optimization:** Minimize bundle sizes and optimize performance by using tree-shaking, code splitting, and lazy loading where applicable.

**3. Security:** Implement security measures to prevent XSS attacks and protect sensitive data by sanitizing inputs and validating user permissions.

**4. Testing:** Write unit tests and end-to-end tests to ensure the reliability and functionality of your Django application with integrated JavaScript frameworks.

**5. Documentation:** Document your integration process and provide clear instructions for other developers to follow when working with JavaScript frameworks in Django.
```

JavaScript frameworks offer powerful tools and libraries for building dynamic and interactive web applications in Django full-stack development. By integrating frameworks like React, Vue.js, and Angular into your Django applications, you can create modern and responsive user interfaces that provide a seamless and engaging experience for your users. With the knowledge and techniques outlined in this guide, you'll be well-equipped to leverage JavaScript frameworks effectively in your Django projects, enhancing the functionality and user experience of your web applications.

Chapter 7

Getting Started with Python: Variables, Data Types, and Control Flow in Django Full Stack Development

Python is a versatile and powerful programming language commonly used in web development, data analysis, artificial intelligence, and more. In Django full-stack development, Python serves as the backend language, handling server-side logic, data processing, and business logic. In this guide, we'll cover the basics of Python programming, including variables, data types, and control flow, with code examples to demonstrate their usage within the context of Django applications.

Introduction to Python

Python is known for its simplicity, readability, and ease of use, making it an ideal language for beginners and experienced developers alike. It features a clean and concise syntax, dynamic typing, and a rich standard library, making it suitable for a wide range of applications.

Variables and Data Types

In Python, variables are containers for storing data values. Unlike statically typed languages, Python variables don't require explicit declaration of data types; instead, the data type is inferred dynamically based on the assigned value.

Example Python Variables and Data Types:

```python
# Integer
age = 30

# Float
height = 1.75

# String
name = "John Doe"

# Boolean
is_student = True

# List
fruits = ["apple", "banana", "orange"]

# Dictionary
person = {"name": "John", "age": 30}
```

Control Flow

Python provides various control flow statements such as `if...else`, `for`, `while`, and `try...except` for controlling the flow of execution based on conditions, looping over iterable objects, and handling exceptions.

Example Python Control Flow:

```python
# if...else Statement
num = 10
if num > 0:
    print("Positive number")
elif num < 0:
    print("Negative number")
else:
    print("Zero")

# for Loop
fruits = ["apple", "banana", "orange"]
for fruit in fruits:
    print(fruit)

# while Loop
counter = 0
while counter < 5:
    print(counter)
```

```
    counter += 1
```

Functions

Functions in Python are reusable blocks of code that perform a specific task. They help in organizing code, promoting code reusability, and improving maintainability.

Example Python Functions:

```python
# Function Definition
def greet(name):
    print("Hello, " + name + "!")

# Function Call
greet("Alice")

# Function with Default Parameter
def multiply(a, b=2):
    return a * b

result = multiply(5)  # Output: 10
```

Integrating Python with Django

In Django full-stack development, Python is used extensively for writing views, models, forms, and business logic. Python scripts are executed on the server-side, handling HTTP requests, processing data, interacting with databases, and rendering dynamic HTML templates.

Example Django View Function:

```python
from django.http import HttpResponse

def index(request):
    return HttpResponse("Hello, Django!")
```

Best Practices for Python Development in Django

1. PEP 8 Style Guide: Follow the Python Enhancement Proposal (PEP) 8 style guide for writing clean, readable, and consistent Python code.

2. Modularization: Organize Python code into modules, packages, and classes to promote code reuse, maintainability, and scalability.

3. Error Handling: Implement error handling mechanisms using try...except blocks to gracefully handle exceptions and errors in Python code.

4. Documentation: Write clear and concise documentation for your Python functions, modules, and classes to facilitate collaboration and maintainability.

5. Testing: Write unit tests and integration tests to ensure the reliability and correctness of your Python code in Django applications.

Python serves as the backbone of Django full-stack development, providing a powerful and versatile language for writing server-side logic, handling data processing, and building web applications. By mastering the basics of Python programming, including variables, data types, control flow, and functions, developers can create robust and scalable Django applications that meet the needs of modern web development. With the knowledge and techniques outlined in this guide, you'll be well-equipped to get started with Python programming in Django and embark on your journey to becoming a proficient Django developer.

Functions, Loops, and Conditionals: Building Reusable Code in Django Full Stack Development

In Django full-stack development, writing clean and efficient code is crucial for building maintainable and scalable web applications. Functions, loops, and conditionals are fundamental building blocks of Python programming and play a significant role in creating reusable and structured code. In this guide, we'll explore how to use functions, loops, and conditionals effectively in Django applications, with code examples to demonstrate their usage and integration within the Django framework.

Functions

Functions in Python are reusable blocks of code that perform a specific task. They help in organizing code, promoting code reusability, and improving maintainability. In Django, functions are commonly used for defining views, utility functions, and business logic.

Example Django View Function:

```python
from django.http import HttpResponse
```

```python
def index(request):
    return HttpResponse("Hello, Django!")
```

Example Utility Function:

```python
def calculate_total_price(quantity, price):
    return quantity * price
```

Example Business Logic Function:

```python
def validate_email(email):
    if "@" in email and "." in email:
        return True
    else:
        return False
```

Loops

Loops in Python allow you to iterate over sequences of data, such as lists, tuples, and dictionaries, and perform operations on each element. Loops are useful for performing repetitive tasks, processing collections of data, and implementing algorithms efficiently.

Example for Loop:

```python
fruits = ["apple", "banana", "orange"]
for fruit in fruits:
    print(fruit)
```

Example While Loop:

```python
counter = 0
while counter < 5:
    print(counter)
    counter += 1
```

Conditionals

Conditionals in Python allow you to execute different blocks of code based on conditions. They are essential for implementing logic, handling edge cases, and controlling the flow of execution in your Django applications.

Example if...else Statement:

```python
num = 10
if num > 0:
    print("Positive number")
elif num < 0:
    print("Negative number")
else:
    print("Zero")
```

Example Ternary Conditional Expression:

```python
is_authenticated = True
message = "Welcome" if is_authenticated else "Please log in"
print(message)
```

Integrating Functions, Loops, and Conditionals in Django

In Django applications, functions, loops, and conditionals are used extensively for defining views, processing data, rendering templates, and implementing business logic. They play a crucial role in building dynamic and interactive web applications that meet the requirements of modern web development.

Example Django View Function with Logic:

```python
from django.http import HttpResponse

def check_age(request, age):
    if age >= 18:
        return HttpResponse("You are eligible to vote")
    else:
        return HttpResponse("You are not eligible to vote")
```

Example Django Template with Loop:

```html
<!DOCTYPE html>
<html lang="en">
<head>
    <meta charset="UTF-8">
    <meta name="viewport" content="width=device-width, initial-scale=1.0">
    <title>Fruits</title>
</head>
<body>
    <ul>
        {% for fruit in fruits %}
            <li>{{ fruit }}</li>
```

```
      {% endfor %}
   </ul>
</body>
</html>
```

Example Django Template with Conditional:

```html
<!DOCTYPE html>
<html lang="en">
<head>
   <meta charset="UTF-8">
   <meta name="viewport" content="width=device-
width, initial-scale=1.0">
   <title>Welcome Message</title>
</head>
<body>
   {% if is_authenticated %}
      <h1>Welcome, {{ username }}</h1>
   {% else %}
      <h1>Please log in</h1>
   {% endif %}
</body>
</html>
```

Best Practices for Building Reusable Code in Django

1. Modularization: Organize code into modules, packages, and functions to promote code reusability and maintainability.

2. DRY Principle: Follow the "Don't Repeat Yourself" principle by avoiding duplicating code and abstracting common functionality into reusable functions.

3. Clear Naming Conventions: Use descriptive and meaningful names for functions, variables, and classes to improve code readability and understanding.

4. Error Handling: Implement error handling mechanisms to handle exceptions gracefully and provide informative error messages to users.

5. Documentation: Write clear and concise documentation for functions, modules, and classes to facilitate collaboration and code maintenance.

Functions, loops, and conditionals are essential building blocks of Python programming in Django full-stack development. By mastering these concepts and integrating them effectively into your Django applications, you can create reusable, efficient, and maintainable code that meets the requirements of modern web development. With the knowledge and techniques outlined in this guide, you'll be well-equipped to write clean, structured, and scalable code in your Django projects, building dynamic and interactive web applications that deliver value to users.

Object-Oriented Programming in Python: Classes and Objects in Django Full Stack Development

Object-Oriented Programming (OOP) is a programming paradigm that focuses on organizing code into classes and objects, allowing for better code organization, reusability, and modularity. In Python, OOP is widely used, and understanding classes and objects is essential for building complex and scalable applications. In this guide, we'll explore the concepts of classes and objects in Python, their usage in Django full-stack development, and provide code examples to illustrate their implementation.

Introduction to Classes and Objects

A class is a blueprint for creating objects, which are instances of that class. Classes define attributes (data) and methods (functions) that represent the behavior of objects. Objects encapsulate data and behavior, providing a way to model real-world entities in code.

Defining Classes in Python

In Python, classes are defined using the `class` keyword, followed by the class name and a colon. Class attributes and methods are defined within the class body using indentation.

Example Python Class:

```python
class Person:
    def __init__(self, name, age):
        self.name = name
        self.age = age

    def greet(self):
        print(f"Hello, my name is {self.name} and I am {self.age} years old.")
```

Creating Objects (Instances) of a Class

Once a class is defined, you can create objects (instances) of that class using the class name followed by parentheses. Objects can have different values for their attributes but share the same behavior defined by the class methods.

Example Creating Objects:

```python
# Create instances of the Person class
person1 = Person("Alice", 30)
person2 = Person("Bob", 25)

# Call methods on objects
person1.greet()  # Output: Hello, my name is Alice and I
am 30 years old.
person2.greet()  # Output: Hello, my name is Bob and I
am 25 years old.
```

Encapsulation and Abstraction

Encapsulation is the bundling of data (attributes) and methods (behavior) within a class, hiding the internal implementation details from the outside world.
Abstraction is the process of exposing only the necessary details of an object while hiding its complexity.

Inheritance and Polymorphism

Inheritance allows a class (subclass) to inherit attributes and methods from another class (superclass), enabling code reuse and promoting modularity. Polymorphism allows objects of different classes to be treated as objects of a common superclass, providing flexibility and extensibility in code.

Usage of Classes and Objects in Django

In Django full-stack development, classes and objects are used extensively for defining models, views, forms, and serializers. Django models represent database tables and are defined as Python classes, with each model class representing a specific data entity.

Example Django Model Class:

```python
from django.db import models

class Product(models.Model):
    name = models.CharField(max_length=100)
    price = models.DecimalField(max_digits=10,
decimal_places=2)
    description = models.TextField()
```

Best Practices for Object-Oriented Programming in Django

1. Class Naming Conventions: Follow naming conventions for classes and methods to ensure clarity and consistency in code.

2. Single Responsibility Principle (SRP): Design classes with a single responsibility to promote modularity and maintainability.

3. Code Reusability: Encapsulate common functionality in reusable classes and methods to avoid code duplication.

4. Composition over Inheritance: Prefer composition over inheritance to build flexible and modular code structures.

5. Unit Testing: Write unit tests for classes and methods to ensure their correctness and functionality in isolation.

Object-oriented programming in Python, with its concepts of classes and objects, is a powerful paradigm for building complex and scalable applications in Django full-stack development. By understanding how to define classes, create objects, and utilize inheritance and polymorphism effectively, developers can create modular, reusable, and maintainable code that meets the requirements of modern web applications. With the knowledge and techniques outlined in this guide, you'll be well-equipped to leverage object-oriented programming principles in your Django projects, building robust and extensible applications that deliver value to users.

Chapter 8

Understanding the Role of Models in Django Full Stack Development

In Django full-stack development, models play a crucial role in defining the structure and behavior of data in web applications. Models represent database tables and provide an abstraction layer for interacting with data, enabling developers to perform CRUD (Create, Read, Update, Delete) operations and define relationships between different data entities. In this guide, we'll explore the role of models in Django, including how to define models, interact with databases, perform queries, and handle relationships, with code examples to illustrate their usage.

Introduction to Models in Django

In Django, models are Python classes that define the structure and behavior of data stored in a database. Each model class represents a database table, with attributes mapping to table columns and methods defining table behavior. Models provide a high-level abstraction for interacting with databases, allowing developers to focus on application logic rather than database management.

Defining Models

Models in Django are defined using the `django.db.models` module, which provides various field types to represent different data types in the database, such as integers, strings, dates, and relationships.

Example Django Model Definition:

```python
from django.db import models

class Product(models.Model):
    name = models.CharField(max_length=100)
    price = models.DecimalField(max_digits=10, decimal_places=2)
    description = models.TextField()
    created_at = models.DateTimeField(auto_now_add=True)
```

Migrations

Once models are defined, Django's migration system allows you to propagate changes to the database schema. Migrations are Python files generated by Django's `makemigrations` command, which represent changes to the database schema such as creating tables, adding columns, or altering constraints.

Example Django Migration:

```bash
$ python manage.py makemigrations
$ python manage.py migrate
```

CRUD Operations

Django models provide a convenient interface for performing CRUD operations on database records. You can create, read, update, and delete records using model methods such as `save()`, `objects.create()`, `objects.get()`, `objects.filter()`, and `delete()`.

Example CRUD Operations:

```python
# Create a new product
product = Product.objects.create(name="Laptop", price=999.99, description="High-performance laptop")

# Retrieve a product by its primary key
product = Product.objects.get(pk=1)
```

```python
# Update a product
product.price = 1099.99
product.save()

# Delete a product
product.delete()
```

Querying Data

Django provides a powerful query API for retrieving data from the database using filters, lookups, aggregations, and annotations. Querysets are lazy-evaluated, allowing you to build complex queries dynamically and optimize database access.

Example Querying Data:

```python
# Retrieve all products
products = Product.objects.all()

# Filter products by price
expensive_products =
Product.objects.filter(price__gte=1000)

# Order products by creation date
```

```
recent_products = Product.objects.order_by('-
created_at')[:5]
```

Relationships

Django models support various types of relationships
between different data entities, such as one-to-one, one-
to-many, and many-to-many relationships. Relationships
are defined using field types such as `ForeignKey`,
`OneToOneField`, and `ManyToManyField`.

Example Relationship Definition:

```python
from django.contrib.auth.models import User

class Order(models.Model):
    user = models.ForeignKey(User,
on_delete=models.CASCADE)
    products = models.ManyToManyField(Product)
    total_price = models.DecimalField(max_digits=10,
decimal_places=2)
```

Best Practices for Using Models in Django

1. Naming Conventions: Follow naming conventions for model classes and fields to ensure clarity and consistency in code.

2. Data Validation: Implement data validation logic in model methods and form validation to ensure data integrity and security.

3. Optimization: Use database indexes, select_related, prefetch_related, and annotate queryset methods to optimize database queries and reduce query times.

4. Atomic Transactions: Use atomic transactions to ensure database integrity and consistency when performing multiple database operations.

5. Testing: Write unit tests and integration tests for model methods and querysets to ensure their correctness and reliability.

Models are a fundamental component of Django full-stack development, providing a powerful abstraction layer for interacting with databases and defining the structure and behavior of data in web applications. By understanding how to define models, perform CRUD operations, query data, handle relationships, and follow best practices, developers can create robust and scalable Django applications that meet the requirements of modern web development. With the knowledge and techniques outlined in this guide, you'll be well-equipped to leverage models effectively in your Django projects, building database-driven web applications that deliver value to users.

Creating Models for User Accounts, Blog Posts, Products, etc. in Django Full Stack Development

In Django full-stack development, creating models is a fundamental step in building database-driven web applications. Models define the structure and behavior of data entities such as user accounts, blog posts, products, and more. By defining models, developers can organize data, perform CRUD operations, and establish relationships between different data entities. In this guide, we'll explore how to create models for user accounts, blog posts, products, and other common data entities in Django, with code examples to illustrate their implementation.

User Accounts Model

User accounts are a fundamental component of most web applications, allowing users to register, log in, and interact with the application's features. In Django, user accounts are managed using the built-in `User` model provided by the `django.contrib.auth` module.

Example User Accounts Model:

```python
from django.contrib.auth.models import User

class UserProfile(models.Model):
    user = models.OneToOneField(User,
on_delete=models.CASCADE)
    bio = models.TextField(blank=True)
    website = models.URLField(blank=True)
```

Blog Posts Model

Blog posts are another common data entity in web applications, allowing users to create, read, update, and delete blog articles. In Django, blog posts can be represented by a model that includes fields for the title, content, author, publication date, and other metadata.

Example Blog Posts Model:

```python
from django.contrib.auth.models import User
```

```python
class BlogPost(models.Model):
    title = models.CharField(max_length=100)
    content = models.TextField()
    author = models.ForeignKey(User,
on_delete=models.CASCADE)
    published_at =
models.DateTimeField(auto_now_add=True)
```

Products Model

Products are often managed in e-commerce and retail applications, allowing users to browse, search, and purchase items. In Django, products can be represented by a model that includes fields for the name, description, price, quantity, and other attributes.

Example Products Model:

```python
class Product(models.Model):
    name = models.CharField(max_length=100)
    description = models.TextField()
    price = models.DecimalField(max_digits=10,
decimal_places=2)
    quantity = models.IntegerField(default=0)
```

Relationships between Models

In Django, relationships between models can be defined using field types such as `ForeignKey`, `OneToOneField`, and `ManyToManyField`. These relationships allow you to establish connections between different data entities, such as users and blog posts, authors and comments, and products and categories.

Example Relationships between Models:

```python
class Comment(models.Model):
    content = models.TextField()
    author = models.ForeignKey(User,
on_delete=models.CASCADE)
    post = models.ForeignKey(BlogPost,
on_delete=models.CASCADE)
    published_at =
models.DateTimeField(auto_now_add=True)
```

Best Practices for Model Design in Django

1. Clarity and Consistency: Follow naming conventions and maintain consistency in model names, field names, and attribute names to ensure clarity and readability in code.

2. Data Validation: Implement data validation logic in model methods and form validation to ensure data integrity and security.

3. Normalization: Follow database normalization principles to reduce redundancy and improve database efficiency by breaking data into smaller, logical units.

4. Optimization: Use database indexes, select_related, prefetch_related, and annotate queryset methods to optimize database queries and reduce query times.

5. Testing: Write unit tests and integration tests for model methods and querysets to ensure their correctness and reliability.

Creating models is a critical step in Django full-stack development, enabling developers to define the structure and behavior of data entities in web applications. By understanding how to create models for user accounts, blog posts, products, and other common data entities, developers can build robust and scalable Django applications that meet the requirements of modern web development. With the knowledge and techniques outlined in this guide, you'll be well-equipped to design and implement models effectively in your Django projects, building database-driven web applications that deliver value to users.

Defining Relationships Between Models: One-to-Many, Many-to-Many in Django Full Stack Development

In Django full-stack development, relationships between models play a crucial role in organizing data and establishing connections between different entities. Two common types of relationships are one-to-many and many-to-many relationships, which allow you to represent complex data structures and create associations between related data entities. In this guide, we'll explore how to define and implement one-to-many and many-to-many relationships between models in Django, with code examples to illustrate their usage and integration within Django applications.

Introduction to Model Relationships in Django

Model relationships in Django allow you to define connections between different data entities, such as users and blog posts, products and categories, and authors and comments. These relationships enable you to represent complex data structures and establish associations between related data entities, facilitating data retrieval, manipulation, and querying.

One-to-Many Relationships

One-to-many relationships are the most common type of relationship in database design, where one record in a table (the "one" side) can be associated with multiple records in another table (the "many" side). In Django, one-to-many relationships are represented using the `ForeignKey` field, which allows you to establish a connection between two models.

Example One-to-Many Relationship:

```python
from django.contrib.auth.models import User

class BlogPost(models.Model):
    title = models.CharField(max_length=100)
    content = models.TextField()
    author = models.ForeignKey(User,
on_delete=models.CASCADE)
    published_at =
models.DateTimeField(auto_now_add=True)
```

In this example, each `BlogPost` is associated with a single `User` (the author), but a single `User` can have multiple `BlogPosts`. The `ForeignKey` field establishes

the one-to-many relationship between the `BlogPost`
model and the `User` model.

Many-to-Many Relationships

Many-to-many relationships occur when multiple
records in one table can be associated with multiple
records in another table. In Django, many-to-many
relationships are represented using the
`ManyToManyField` field, which allows you to create a
many-to-many relationship between two models.

Example Many-to-Many Relationship:

```python
class Product(models.Model):
    name = models.CharField(max_length=100)
    description = models.TextField()
    categories = models.ManyToManyField('Category')
```

In this example, each `Product` can be associated with
multiple `Category` objects, and each `Category` can be
associated with multiple `Product` objects. The
`ManyToManyField` field establishes the many-to-many
relationship between the `Product` model and the
`Category` model.

Handling Related Objects

Once relationships are defined between models, Django provides a convenient way to access related objects using model attributes and querysets. You can retrieve related objects, create new relationships, and filter objects based on related fields.

Example Accessing Related Objects:

```python
# Get all blog posts written by a specific user
user = User.objects.get(username='alice')
blog_posts = user.blogpost_set.all()

# Add a category to a product
product = Product.objects.get(pk=1)
category = Category.objects.get(pk=1)
product.categories.add(category)

# Filter products by category
category = Category.objects.get(name='Electronics')
products = Product.objects.filter(categories=category)
```

Best Practices for Defining Model Relationships in Django

1. Clear Naming Conventions: Follow naming conventions for related fields and attributes to ensure clarity and consistency in code.

2. Data Integrity: Ensure data integrity by specifying appropriate `on_delete` behavior for `ForeignKey` fields and avoiding orphaned records.

3. Optimization: Use `select_related` and `prefetch_related` queryset methods to optimize database queries and reduce query times when accessing related objects.

4. Testing: Write unit tests and integration tests to verify the correctness and functionality of model relationships and related operations.

Defining relationships between models is a fundamental aspect of Django full-stack development, enabling you to organize data and establish connections between different data entities. By understanding how to define and implement one-to-many and many-to-many relationships between models, developers can build robust and scalable Django applications that meet the requirements of modern web development. With the knowledge and techniques outlined in this guide, you'll be well-equipped to leverage model relationships effectively in your Django projects, creating database-driven web applications that deliver value to users.

Model Admin: Managing Your Website's Data with Ease in Django Full Stack Development

In Django full-stack development, the Model Admin interface provides a powerful tool for managing website data with ease. Model Admin allows developers to create a user-friendly administrative interface for interacting with database models, performing CRUD operations, managing relationships, and configuring advanced features such as search, filtering, and permissions. In this guide, we'll explore how to use Model Admin in Django applications, with code examples to illustrate its usage and integration within the Django framework.

Introduction to Model Admin in Django

Model Admin is a built-in feature of Django's admin site, which is a customizable interface for managing website data. Model Admin allows developers to define custom administration panels for each registered model, providing a convenient way to interact with database records without writing custom views or templates.

Registering Models with Model Admin

To enable Model Admin for a Django model, you need to register the model with the admin site using the `admin.site.register()` function. This function takes two arguments: the model class and an optional admin class that customizes the appearance and behavior of the admin interface.

Example Registering Models with Model Admin:

```python
from django.contrib import admin
from .models import Product, Category

@admin.register(Product)
class ProductAdmin(admin.ModelAdmin):
    list_display = ('name', 'price', 'quantity')

@admin.register(Category)
class CategoryAdmin(admin.ModelAdmin):
    list_display = ('name',)
```

Customizing Model Admin Interface

Model Admin allows you to customize various aspects of the administrative interface, including the list display, search fields, filters, fields ordering, fieldsets, and more.

These customizations help to create a user-friendly interface tailored to the specific requirements of your application.

Example Customizing Model Admin Interface:

```python
class ProductAdmin(admin.ModelAdmin):
    list_display = ('name', 'price', 'quantity')
    search_fields = ('name',)
    list_filter = ('category',)
    ordering = ('name',)
    fieldsets = (
        (None, {
            'fields': ('name', 'description', 'price', 'quantity')
        }),
        ('Advanced options', {
            'classes': ('collapse',),
            'fields': ('category',),
        }),
```

Handling Relationships in Model Admin

Model Admin allows you to handle relationships between models and display related objects within the administrative interface. You can use inline models, which are displayed as nested forms within the parent model, to manage one-to-many and many-to-many relationships easily.

Example Handling Relationships in Model Admin:

```python
from .models import Product, Category

class ProductInline(admin.TabularInline):
    model = Product

@admin.register(Category)
class CategoryAdmin(admin.ModelAdmin):
    inlines = [
        ProductInline,
    ]
```

Advanced Features of Model Admin

Model Admin provides several advanced features to enhance the functionality and usability of the administrative interface. These features include permissions, actions, readonly fields, custom form validation, custom list filters, and more.

Example Advanced Features of Model Admin:

```python
class ProductAdmin(admin.ModelAdmin):
    readonly_fields = ('created_at', 'updated_at')
    actions = ['make_discounted', 'make_featured']
    list_filter = ('category', 'is_featured')

    def make_discounted(self, request, queryset):
        queryset.update(discounted=True)
    make_discounted.short_description = "Mark selected products as discounted"

    def make_featured(self, request, queryset):
        queryset.update(is_featured=True)
    make_featured.short_description = "Mark selected products as featured"
```

Best Practices for Using Model Admin in Django

1. Security: Secure the admin interface by restricting access to authorized users and configuring permissions and authentication mechanisms.

2. Customization: Customize the admin interface to match the design and functionality requirements of your application, including branding, styling, and layout.

3. Optimization: Optimize the performance of the admin interface by limiting the number of displayed records, optimizing queries, and using caching mechanisms.

4. Testing: Test the functionality and usability of the admin interface using automated tests and user acceptance testing to ensure its correctness and reliability.

Model Admin is a powerful tool for managing website data with ease in Django full-stack development. By leveraging Model Admin, developers can create a user-friendly administrative interface for interacting with database models, performing CRUD operations, managing relationships, and configuring advanced features. With the knowledge and techniques outlined in this guide, you'll be well-equipped to use Model Admin effectively in your Django projects, creating a seamless data management experience for administrators and content managers.

Chapter 9

Understanding the Role of Views in Django Full Stack Development

In Django full-stack development, views play a crucial role in handling user requests, processing data, and generating responses. Views serve as the bridge between the front end and the back end of a web application, orchestrating the interaction between the user interface and the underlying data models. In this guide, we'll explore the role of views in Django, including how to define views, handle different types of requests, implement business logic, and render templates, with code examples to illustrate their usage and integration within the Django framework.

Introduction to Views in Django

Views in Django are Python functions or classes that receive HTTP requests from clients, process data as needed, and return HTTP responses. Views encapsulate the logic for handling specific URL patterns and implementing the business logic of web applications. Django's URL routing mechanism maps URLs to views, allowing developers to create clean and modular code structures.

Defining Views

Views in Django can be defined as functions or classes, depending on the complexity and requirements of the application. Function-based views are simpler and suitable for handling basic logic, while class-based views provide additional features such as mixins, inheritance, and built-in methods for handling common tasks.

Example Function-Based View:

```python
from django.http import HttpResponse

def hello(request):
    return HttpResponse("Hello, Django!")
```

Example Class-Based View:

```python
from django.http import HttpResponse
from django.views import View

class HelloView(View):
    def get(self, request):
        return HttpResponse("Hello, Django!")
```

```
```

Handling Requests

Views in Django can handle different types of HTTP requests, such as GET, POST, PUT, DELETE, and more. Depending on the HTTP method used, views can perform different actions, such as retrieving data, creating new records, updating existing records, or deleting records.

Example Handling GET Request:

```python
from django.http import HttpResponse

def get_product(request, product_id):
    # Retrieve product from database
    product = Product.objects.get(pk=product_id)
    # Render product details template
    return render(request, 'product_details.html',
{'product': product})
```

Example Handling POST Request:

```python
from django.http import HttpResponse
```

```python
def create_product(request):
    if request.method == 'POST':
        # Process form data and create new product
        form = ProductForm(request.POST)
        if form.is_valid():
            form.save()
            return HttpResponse("Product created successfully")
    else:
        form = ProductForm()
    return render(request, 'create_product.html', {'form': form})
```

Implementing Business Logic

Views in Django are responsible for implementing the business logic of web applications, including data validation, form processing, authentication, authorization, and more. Views interact with models, forms, and other components to perform operations on data and enforce application logic.

Example Implementing Business Logic:

```python
from django.shortcuts import redirect
```

```python
from django.contrib.auth.decorators import
login_required

@login_required
def add_to_cart(request, product_id):
    product = Product.objects.get(pk=product_id)
    # Add product to user's shopping cart
    cart.add(product)
    return redirect('cart')
```

Rendering Templates

Views in Django can render HTML templates to
generate dynamic web pages and provide a user-friendly
interface for interacting with web applications.
Templates are typically rendered using the `render()`
function, which takes a template name and a context
dictionary as arguments.

Example Rendering Templates:

```python
from django.shortcuts import render

def home(request):
    products = Product.objects.all()
```

```
    return render(request, 'home.html', {'products':
products})
```

Best Practices for Writing Views in Django

1. Separation of Concerns: Keep views focused on handling requests and implementing business logic, avoiding mixing presentation logic within views.

2. Modularity: Break down complex views into smaller, reusable functions or classes to promote modularity and maintainability.

3. Error Handling: Implement error handling mechanisms to gracefully handle exceptions and provide informative error messages to users.

4. Authentication and Authorization: Use Django's built-in authentication and authorization mechanisms to secure views and restrict access to authenticated users as needed.

5. Unit Testing: Write unit tests for views to ensure their correctness and functionality, covering different scenarios and edge cases.

Views are a fundamental component of Django full-stack development, serving as the backbone of web applications by handling user requests, processing data, and generating responses. By understanding the role of views and following best practices for writing views in Django, developers can create clean, modular, and maintainable code structures that meet the requirements of modern web development. With the knowledge and techniques outlined in this guide, you'll be well-equipped to leverage views effectively in your Django projects, building dynamic and interactive web applications that deliver value to users.

Creating Function-Based Views for Simple Interactions in Django Full Stack Development

Function-based views are a fundamental aspect of Django web development, providing a simple and concise way to handle HTTP requests, process data, and generate responses. In this guide, we'll explore how to create function-based views in Django for handling simple interactions such as displaying information, processing form submissions, and performing basic CRUD operations. We'll provide code examples to illustrate the implementation of function-based views and their integration within Django applications.

Introduction to Function-Based Views in Django

Function-based views are Python functions that take an HTTP request as input and return an HTTP response. These views encapsulate the logic for handling specific URL patterns and implementing the functionality of web applications. Function-based views are flexible, easy to understand, and suitable for handling simple interactions in Django applications.

Creating Basic Function-Based Views

To create a function-based view in Django, you define a Python function that takes an `HttpRequest` object as its parameter and returns an `HttpResponse` object. Inside the view function, you can access request data, process it as needed, and generate a response to be sent back to the client.

Example Basic Function-Based View:

```python
from django.http import HttpResponse

def hello_world(request):
    return HttpResponse("Hello, Django!")
```

In this example, the `hello_world` function is a basic function-based view that returns a simple HTTP response with the text "Hello, Django!".

Handling HTTP Methods

Function-based views in Django can handle different types of HTTP methods, such as GET, POST, PUT, DELETE, and more. You can use conditional statements to execute different logic based on the HTTP method used in the request.

Example Handling GET and POST Requests:

```python
from django.http import HttpResponse
from django.shortcuts import render

def form_view(request):
    if request.method == 'GET':
        # Render form template for GET requests
        return render(request, 'form.html')
    elif request.method == 'POST':
        # Process form data for POST requests
        name = request.POST.get('name')
        return HttpResponse(f"Hello, {name}!")
```

In this example, the `form_view` function-based view renders a form template for GET requests and processes form data for POST requests.

Integrating with Templates

Function-based views in Django often render HTML templates to generate dynamic web pages and provide a user-friendly interface for interacting with web applications. You can use the `render()` function to render templates and pass data to the template context.

Example Rendering Template in Function-Based View:

```python
from django.shortcuts import render

def home(request):
    products = Product.objects.all()
    return render(request, 'home.html', {'products': products})
```

In this example, the `home` function-based view retrieves a list of products from the database and passes it to the `home.html` template for rendering.

Handling Form Submissions

Function-based views are commonly used to handle form submissions in Django applications. You can access form data from the request object, validate it, and process it as needed.

Example Handling Form Submissions in Function-Based View:

```python
from django.http import HttpResponse
from django.shortcuts import render

def contact_form(request):
    if request.method == 'POST':
        name = request.POST.get('name')
        email = request.POST.get('email')
        message = request.POST.get('message')
        # Process form data
        return HttpResponse("Thank you for your message!")
    else:
        return render(request, 'contact_form.html')
```

In this example, the `contact_form` function-based view handles form submissions by retrieving form data from the request object and processing it accordingly.

Best Practices for Function-Based Views in Django

1. Separation of Concerns: Keep views focused on handling specific interactions and avoid mixing unrelated logic within view functions.

2. Code Reusability: Factor out common functionality into separate functions or modules to promote code reusability and maintainability.

3. Error Handling: Implement error handling mechanisms to gracefully handle exceptions and provide informative error messages to users.

4. Testing: Write unit tests for function-based views to ensure their correctness and functionality, covering different scenarios and edge cases.

Function-based views are a versatile and efficient way to handle simple interactions in Django full-stack development. By creating function-based views, you can handle HTTP requests, process data, render templates, and provide a user-friendly interface for interacting with web applications. With the knowledge and techniques outlined in this guide, you'll be well-equipped to leverage function-based views effectively in your Django projects, building dynamic and interactive web applications that deliver value to users.

Building Class-Based Views for More Complex Logic in Django Full Stack Development

Class-based views (CBVs) are a powerful feature of Django that allow developers to organize and reuse code more efficiently, especially for handling complex logic and interactions within web applications. In this guide, we'll explore how to create class-based views in Django, including their benefits, structure, and implementation for various scenarios. We'll provide code examples to illustrate the usage and integration of class-based views within Django applications.

Introduction to Class-Based Views in Django

Class-based views are Python classes that encapsulate the logic for handling HTTP requests and generating responses. Unlike function-based views, which are simple functions, class-based views provide a more structured and object-oriented approach to handling views in Django applications. Class-based views offer several advantages, including code reuse, modularity, and easier organization of complex logic.

Creating Basic Class-Based Views

To create a class-based view in Django, you define a Python class that inherits from one of Django's built-in view classes. Django provides a variety of view classes for different types of interactions, such as displaying data, processing form submissions, handling AJAX requests, and more.

Example Basic Class-Based View:

```python
from django.views import View
from django.http import HttpResponse

class HelloWorldView(View):
    def get(self, request):
        return HttpResponse("Hello, Django!")
```

In this example, the `HelloWorldView` class-based view defines a `get()` method to handle GET requests and return a simple HTTP response with the text "Hello, Django!".

Handling Different HTTP Methods

Class-based views in Django can handle different types of HTTP methods, such as GET, POST, PUT, DELETE, and more. You can implement methods corresponding to different HTTP methods to execute specific logic based on the type of request.

Example Handling GET and POST Requests:

```python
from django.views import View
from django.shortcuts import render
from .forms import ContactForm

class ContactFormView(View):
    def get(self, request):
        form = ContactForm()
        return render(request, 'contact_form.html', {'form': form})

    def post(self, request):
        form = ContactForm(request.POST)
        if form.is_valid():
            # Process valid form data
            return HttpResponse("Thank you for your message!")
        else:
```

```
        # Handle invalid form submission
        return render(request, 'contact_form.html',
{'form': form})
```

In this example, the `ContactFormView` class-based view defines `get()` and `post()` methods to handle GET and POST requests, respectively. The `get()` method renders a form template for displaying the contact form, while the `post()` method processes form submissions and validates the form data.

Integrating with Templates

Class-based views in Django often render HTML templates to generate dynamic web pages and provide a user-friendly interface for interacting with web applications. You can override the `get()` method to render templates and pass data to the template context.

Example Rendering Template in Class-Based View:

```python
from django.views.generic import TemplateView

class HomeView(TemplateView):
    template_name = 'home.html'
```

```
def get_context_data(self, kwargs):
    context = super().get_context_data(kwargs)
    context['products'] = Product.objects.all()
    return context
```

In this example, the `HomeView` class-based view
inherits from `TemplateView` and overrides the
`get_context_data()` method to pass a list of products to
the template context. The `template_name` attribute
specifies the name of the template to render.

Handling Form Submissions with FormViews

Django provides specialized class-based views called
FormViews for handling form submissions and
processing form data. FormViews encapsulate common
form-related logic, such as form validation, form
rendering, form processing, and form redirection.

Example FormView for Handling Form Submissions:

```python
from django.views.generic import FormView
from .forms import ContactForm

class ContactFormView(FormView):
    template_name = 'contact_form.html'
```

```
    form_class = ContactForm
    success_url = '/thank-you/'

    def form_valid(self, form):
        # Process valid form data
        return super().form_valid(form)
```

In this example, the `ContactFormView` class-based view inherits from `FormView` and specifies the form template, form class, and success URL. The `form_valid()` method is called when the form submission is valid, allowing you to process the form data.

Best Practices for Using Class-Based Views in Django

1. Modularity: Break down complex logic into separate methods within class-based views to promote modularity and maintainability.

2. Code Reusability: Reuse common functionality by inheriting from built-in view classes and leveraging mixins and inheritance.

3. Error Handling: Implement error handling mechanisms within class-based views to gracefully handle exceptions and provide informative error messages to users.

4. Testing: Write unit tests for class-based views to ensure their correctness and functionality, covering different scenarios and edge cases.

Class-based views are a powerful feature of Django full-stack development that allow developers to organize and reuse code more efficiently, especially for handling complex logic and interactions within web applications. By creating class-based views, you can encapsulate view logic in a structured and object-oriented manner, leading to cleaner, more maintainable code. With the knowledge and techniques outlined in this guide, you'll be well-equipped to leverage class-based views effectively in your Django projects, building dynamic and interactive web applications that deliver value to users.

Handling Different HTTP Methods (GET, POST, etc.) in Django Full Stack Development

In Django full-stack development, handling different HTTP methods is a fundamental aspect of building web applications. HTTP methods such as GET, POST, PUT, DELETE, and others are used to perform various actions on resources and interact with web servers. In this guide, we'll explore how to handle different HTTP methods in Django views, including examples of GET and POST requests, along with code snippets to illustrate their implementation within Django applications.

Introduction to HTTP Methods

HTTP (Hypertext Transfer Protocol) defines several methods that indicate the desired action to be performed on a resource. The most commonly used HTTP methods are:

- **GET**: Retrieve data from the server.

- **POST**: Send data to the server to create or update a resource.

- **PUT**: Update an existing resource on the server.

- **DELETE**: Remove a resource from the server.

- **PATCH**: Partially update a resource on the server.

- **HEAD**: Retrieve metadata about a resource without fetching the resource itself.

In Django, views are responsible for handling incoming HTTP requests and generating appropriate responses based on the requested method.

Handling GET Requests

GET requests are used to retrieve data from the server. In Django, you can define a view function or class-based view to handle GET requests by implementing the `get()` method.

Example Function-Based View Handling GET Request:

```python
from django.http import JsonResponse

def get_data(request):
    data = {'message': 'This is a GET request'}
    return JsonResponse(data)
```

Example Class-Based View Handling GET Request:

```python
from django.http import JsonResponse
from django.views import View
```

```python
class GetDataView(View):
    def get(self, request):
        data = {'message': 'This is a GET request'}
        return JsonResponse(data)
```

Handling POST Requests

POST requests are used to send data to the server, typically to create or update a resource. In Django, you can define a view function or class-based view to handle POST requests by implementing the `post()` method.

Example Function-Based View Handling POST Request:

```python
from django.http import JsonResponse

def create_data(request):
    if request.method == 'POST':
        data = request.POST.get('data')
        # Process data and create resource
        return JsonResponse({'message': 'Resource created successfully'})
    else:
        return JsonResponse({'error': 'POST method required'})
```

```
```

Example Class-Based View Handling POST Request:

```python
from django.http import JsonResponse
from django.views import View

class CreateDataView(View):
    def post(self, request):
        data = request.POST.get('data')
        # Process data and create resource
        return JsonResponse({'message': 'Resource created successfully'})
```

Handling Other HTTP Methods

Django views can handle other HTTP methods such as PUT, DELETE, PATCH, HEAD, and more by implementing the corresponding methods (`put()`, `delete()`, `patch()`, `head()`, etc.) in class-based views or using conditional statements in function-based views.

Example Handling PUT Request in Class-Based View:

```python
```

```
from django.http import JsonResponse
from django.views import View

class UpdateDataView(View):
    def put(self, request):
        data = request.PUT.get('data')
        # Process data and update resource
        return JsonResponse({'message': 'Resource updated successfully'})
```

Best Practices for Handling Different HTTP Methods in Django

1. Consistent API Design: Follow RESTful principles and maintain consistency in handling HTTP methods across views and endpoints.

2. Input Validation: Validate input data from requests to ensure data integrity and security.

3. Error Handling: Implement error handling mechanisms to handle unexpected situations and provide informative error messages to clients.

4. Testing: Write unit tests for views to verify their correctness and functionality, covering different scenarios and edge cases for each HTTP method.

Handling different HTTP methods is essential in Django full-stack development for building robust and scalable web applications. By properly implementing views to handle GET, POST, PUT, DELETE, and other HTTP methods, developers can create RESTful APIs and interactive web interfaces that meet the requirements of modern web development. With the knowledge and techniques outlined in this guide, you'll be well-equipped to handle different HTTP methods effectively in your Django projects, ensuring smooth communication between clients and servers and delivering a seamless user experience.

Passing Data Between Views and Templates in Django Full Stack Development

In Django full-stack development, passing data between views and templates is a common task essential for building dynamic and interactive web applications. Views retrieve data from the database or other sources and pass it to templates for rendering, where it can be displayed to users. In this guide, we'll explore various methods for passing data between views and templates in Django, including using context dictionaries, template context processors, and template tags, with code examples to illustrate their implementation within Django applications.

Introduction to Passing Data Between Views and Templates

Django follows the MVC (Model-View-Template) architectural pattern, where views handle business logic, templates handle presentation logic, and models represent data structures. To display dynamic content in templates, data must be passed from views to templates. Django provides several mechanisms for passing data, allowing developers to choose the most suitable approach based on the requirements of their application.

Using Context Dictionaries

One of the simplest and most common methods for passing data from views to templates in Django is using context dictionaries. Context dictionaries are dictionaries containing key-value pairs representing data to be passed to templates. Views pass context dictionaries to templates when rendering them.

Example Using Context Dictionaries:

```python
from django.shortcuts import render

def my_view(request):
```

```
    data = {'name': 'John', 'age': 30}
    return render(request, 'my_template.html',
context=data)
```

In this example, the `my_view` function-based view passes a context dictionary containing data to the `my_template.html` template when rendering it.

Using Template Context Processors

Template context processors are functions that add data to the template context globally for all templates rendered in a Django application. Django provides several built-in context processors, and developers can also define custom context processors to add custom data to the template context.

Example Using Built-in Template Context Processor:

```python
# settings.py

TEMPLATES = [
    {
        'OPTIONS': {
            'context_processors': [
                ...
```

```
        'django.template.context_processors.request',
```

In this example, the built-in
`django.template.context_processors.request` context
processor adds the `request` object to the template
context, allowing access to request data in templates.

Using Template Tags

Template tags are special syntax constructs used within
templates to perform logic, iterate over data, or display
dynamic content. Django provides built-in template tags
for accessing and rendering data passed from views to
templates via context dictionaries.

Example Using Template Tags:

```html
<!-- my_template.html -->

<h1>Hello, {{ name }}</h1>
<p>Your age is {{ age }}</p>
```

In this example, the `{{ name }}` and `{{ age }}`
template tags are used to access and display the `name`
and `age` data passed from the view.

Using Class-Based Views with ContextMixin

When using class-based views (CBVs) in Django, the `ContextMixin` class can be used to pass data to templates by adding it to the template context. CBVs inherit from `ContextMixin` and use the `get_context_data()` method to add data to the context dictionary.

Example Using Class-Based Views with ContextMixin:

```python
from django.views.generic import TemplateView

class MyView(TemplateView):
    template_name = 'my_template.html'

    def get_context_data(self, kwargs):
        context = super().get_context_data(kwargs)
        context['name'] = 'John'
        context['age'] = 30
        return context
```

In this example, the `MyView` class-based view inherits from `TemplateView` and overrides the `get_context_data()` method to add the `name` and `age` data to the template context.

Best Practices for Passing Data Between Views and Templates

1. Keep Views Lean: Avoid performing heavy data processing or business logic in views. Instead, move such logic to models or utility functions and pass the results to views for rendering.

2. Separation of Concerns: Keep presentation logic separate from business logic. Templates should focus on rendering data, while views should handle data retrieval and processing.

3. Use Context Processors Sparingly: Only use context processors for data that needs to be available in all templates across the application. Overusing context processors can lead to bloated template contexts.

4. Template Tags for Logic: Use template tags to perform simple logic or iterate over data within templates. For more complex logic, consider moving it to views or custom template tags.

Passing data between views and templates is a fundamental aspect of Django full-stack development for building dynamic and interactive web applications. By using context dictionaries, template context processors, template tags, and class-based views with `ContextMixin`, developers can effectively pass data from views to templates and render dynamic content to users. With the knowledge and techniques outlined in this guide, you'll be well-equipped to pass data between views and templates efficiently in your Django projects, delivering engaging and personalized user experiences.

Chapter 10

Introduction to Django's Template Language in Django Full Stack Development

Django's template language is a powerful tool for building dynamic and interactive web applications. It provides a simple yet robust syntax for generating HTML dynamically, handling conditional logic, looping over data, and performing other operations within templates. In this guide, we'll explore the basics of Django's template language, including its syntax, built-in tags and filters, variable rendering, template inheritance, and more, with code examples to illustrate its usage within Django applications.

Overview of Django's Template Language

Django's template language is designed to make it easy to build web pages dynamically by combining static HTML with dynamic content generated from data provided by views. Templates are HTML files containing template tags, which are special syntax constructs that perform various operations such as rendering variables, controlling flow with conditional statements and loops, including other templates, and more.

Variable Rendering

One of the core features of Django's template language is the ability to render variables dynamically within templates. Variables can be rendered using double curly braces (`{{ variable }}`), and their values are replaced with the corresponding data provided by views.

Example of Variable Rendering:

```html
<!-- template.html -->
<h1>Hello, {{ name }}</h1>
<p>Your age is {{ age }}</p>
```

In this example, the `name` and `age` variables are rendered dynamically within the HTML template, displaying the values provided by the view.

Template Tags

Template tags are special syntax constructs used within templates to perform logic, control flow, and output dynamic content. Django provides a variety of built-in template tags for common tasks such as looping over data, rendering conditional statements, including other templates, and more.

Example of Using Template Tags:

```html
<!-- template.html -->
<ul>
{% for item in items %}
   <li>{{ item }}</li>
{% endfor %}
</ul>
```

In this example, the `{% for %}` template tag is used to loop over a list of items and render each item dynamically within an HTML list.

Template Filters

Template filters are functions that modify the output of template variables or tags. Django provides a set of built-in template filters for common tasks such as formatting dates, converting text to uppercase or lowercase, truncating text, and more.

Example of Using Template Filters:

```html
<!-- template.html -->
<p>{{ text|lower }}</p>
<p>{{ date|date:"F d, Y" }}</p>
```

In this example, the `lower` filter is applied to the `text` variable to convert it to lowercase, and the `date` filter is applied to the `date` variable to format it as a full month name followed by the day and year.

Template Inheritance

Template inheritance is a powerful feature of Django's template language that allows developers to create reusable and modular templates by defining a base template with common elements and extending it in child templates with additional content.

Example of Template Inheritance:

```html
<!-- base.html -->
<!DOCTYPE html>
<html lang="en">
<head>
    <meta charset="UTF-8">
```

```
    <title>{% block title %}My Website{% endblock
%}</title>
</head>
<body>
  <header>
    <h1>My Website</h1>
  </header>
  <nav>
    <ul>
      <li><a href="/">Home</a></li>
      <li><a href="/about/">About</a></li>
      <li><a href="/contact/">Contact</a></li>
    </ul>
  </nav>
  <main>
    {% block content %}
    {% endblock %}
  </main>
  <footer>
    <p>&copy; 2024 My Website</p>
  </footer>
</body>
</html>
```

```html
<!-- child.html -->
{% extends "base.html" %}
```

```
{% block title %}About Us{% endblock %}

{% block content %}
    <h2>About Us</h2>
    <p>Welcome to our website! We are a team of
developers passionate about Django.</p>
{% endblock %}
```

In this example, the `child.html` template extends the `base.html` template and overrides the `title` and `content` blocks with custom content.

Best Practices for Using Django's Template Language

1. Keep Templates Simple: Avoid adding complex logic or business logic in templates. Templates should focus on presentation logic and rendering data provided by views.

2. Use Template Inheritance: Use template inheritance to create reusable and modular templates, reducing duplication and improving maintainability.

3. Optimize Performance: Minimize the use of expensive template tags and filters, especially in loops or high-traffic areas of the application, to improve performance.

4. Organize Templates: Organize templates into logical directories and use descriptive names to make it easier to navigate and maintain the template structure.

Django's template language is a powerful tool for building dynamic and interactive web applications in Django full-stack development. By mastering the basics of Django's template language, including variable rendering, template tags, filters, and template inheritance, developers can create clean, modular, and maintainable templates that effectively render dynamic content to users. With the knowledge and techniques outlined in this guide, you'll be well-equipped to leverage Django's template language effectively in your Django projects, delivering engaging and user-friendly web interfaces.

Displaying Model Data with Template Tags and Filters in Django Full Stack Development

In Django full-stack development, displaying model data in templates is a common task essential for building dynamic and interactive web applications. Django provides powerful tools, including template tags and filters, to efficiently render model data within templates.

In this guide, we'll explore how to display model data using template tags and filters in Django, including examples of accessing model attributes, iterating over querysets, filtering and ordering data, and more, with code examples to illustrate their implementation within Django applications.

Introduction to Displaying Model Data in Templates

Django's template language allows developers to access and display data stored in models within HTML templates. Models represent the structure of database tables and define the fields and relationships between data entities. Template tags and filters provide convenient ways to interact with model data, retrieve specific objects or querysets, filter and order data, and perform other operations within templates.

Accessing Model Attributes

To display model data in templates, you can use template tags to access model attributes and render their values dynamically within HTML elements.

Example of Accessing Model Attributes:

```html
<!-- template.html -->
```

```html
<h1>{{ article.title }}</h1>
<p>{{ article.content }}</p>
```

In this example, the `article` object represents an instance of a model, and its `title` and `content` attributes are rendered dynamically within the HTML template.

Iterating Over Querysets

Querysets are lists of objects retrieved from the database using Django's ORM (Object-Relational Mapping). You can use template tags to iterate over querysets and render each object's attributes within HTML elements.

Example of Iterating Over Querysets:

```html
<!-- template.html -->
<ul>
{% for article in articles %}
    <li>{{ article.title }}</li>
{% endfor %}
</ul>
```

In this example, the `{% for %}` template tag is used to loop over a queryset of `article` objects and render the `title` attribute of each article within an HTML list item.

Filtering and Ordering Data

Django's ORM provides powerful query capabilities for filtering and ordering data retrieved from the database. You can use template tags to filter querysets based on specific criteria and order them as needed before rendering in templates.

Example of Filtering and Ordering Data:

```html
<!-- template.html -->
<ul>
{% for article in articles|slice:":5" %}
   <li>{{ article.title }}</li>
{% endfor %}
</ul>
```

In this example, the `slice` filter is used to limit the queryset to the first five articles, effectively filtering the data before rendering it in the template.

Using Template Tags for Complex Logic

Template tags can be used to perform more complex logic within templates, such as conditional statements, including other templates, or executing custom template tags and filters.

Example of Using Template Tags for Complex Logic:

```html
<!-- template.html -->
{% if articles %}
  <ul>
  {% for article in articles %}
    <li>{{ article.title }}</li>
  {% endfor %}
  </ul>
{% else %}
  <p>No articles found.</p>
{% endif %}
```

In this example, the `{% if %}` template tag is used to conditionally render a list of articles if they exist, or display a message if no articles are found.

Best Practices for Displaying Model Data in Templates

1. Keep Templates Lean: Minimize the amount of logic and business logic in templates. Templates should focus on presentation logic and rendering data provided by views.

2. Use Querysets Wisely: Optimize querysets to retrieve only the necessary data from the database and avoid unnecessary database queries or fetching excessive amounts of data.

3. Cache Frequently Accessed Data: Cache frequently accessed or expensive data to improve performance and reduce database load.

4. Organize Templates: Organize templates into logical directories and use descriptive names to make it easier to navigate and maintain the template structure.

Displaying model data with template tags and filters is a fundamental aspect of Django full-stack development for building dynamic and interactive web applications. By leveraging Django's powerful template language and ORM capabilities, developers can efficiently render model data within HTML templates, providing users with engaging and personalized web experiences. With the knowledge and techniques outlined in this guide, you'll be well-equipped to display model data effectively in your Django projects, delivering compelling and user-friendly web interfaces.

Creating Reusable Templates and Extending Layouts in Django Full Stack Development

In Django full-stack development, creating reusable templates and extending layouts is a fundamental practice for building modular, maintainable, and scalable web applications. Django's template language provides powerful tools for defining base templates with common elements and extending them in child templates to add specific content. In this guide, we'll explore how to create reusable templates, extend layout templates, use template inheritance, and implement modular template structures in Django applications, with code examples to illustrate their implementation.

Introduction to Reusable Templates and Layouts

Reusable templates and layouts allow developers to define common elements, such as headers, footers, navigation menus, and other structural components, in base templates and reuse them across multiple pages in a Django application. This approach promotes code reusability, modularity, and consistency, leading to cleaner and more maintainable codebases.

Defining Base Templates

Base templates serve as the foundation for other templates in a Django application, providing a layout structure and common elements shared across multiple pages. Base templates typically include HTML markup, CSS stylesheets, JavaScript scripts, and other assets required for rendering web pages.

Example of a Base Template:

```html
<!-- base.html -->
<!DOCTYPE html>
<html lang="en">
<head>
    <meta charset="UTF-8">
    <title>{% block title %}My Website{% endblock %}</title>
    <link rel="stylesheet" href="{% static 'css/styles.css' %}">
</head>
<body>
    <header>
        <h1>My Website</h1>
    </header>
    <nav>
        <ul>
```

```
        <li><a href="/">Home</a></li>
        <li><a href="/about/">About</a></li>
        <li><a href="/contact/">Contact</a></li>
      </ul>
    </nav>
    <main>
      {% block content %}
      {% endblock %}
    </main>
    <footer>
      <p>&copy; 2024 My Website</p>
    </footer>
  </body>
</html>
```
```

In this example, the `base.html` template defines the
basic structure of the website, including a header,
navigation menu, main content area, and footer. It also
includes a block named `content` where child templates
can insert specific content.

## Extending Base Templates

Child templates extend base templates by inheriting their
structure and overriding specific blocks with custom
content. Child templates only need to define the content
```

unique to their pages, while the common layout and structural elements are inherited from the base template.

Example of Extending a Base Template:

```html
<!-- child.html -->
{% extends "base.html" %}

{% block title %}About Us{% endblock %}

{% block content %}
    <h2>About Us</h2>
    <p>Welcome to our website! We are a team of developers passionate about Django.</p>
{% endblock %}
```

In this example, the `child.html` template extends the `base.html` template and overrides the `title` and `content` blocks with custom content specific to the "About Us" page.

Using Template Inheritance for Modularization

Template inheritance allows developers to create modular and reusable templates by breaking down complex layouts into smaller components and inheriting them in parent templates as needed. This approach promotes code reusability and simplifies maintenance by separating concerns and isolating changes to specific template components.

Example of Modular Template Inheritance:

```html
<!-- header.html -->
<header>
   <h1>My Website</h1>
</header>
```

```html
<!-- footer.html -->
<footer>
   <p>&copy; 2024 My Website</p>
</footer>
```

```html
<!-- base.html -->
<!DOCTYPE html>
<html lang="en">
<head>
   <meta charset="UTF-8">
```

```html
<title>{% block title %}My Website{% endblock %}</title>
    <link rel="stylesheet" href="{% static 'css/styles.css' %}">
</head>
<body>
    {% include 'header.html' %}
    <nav>
      <ul>
        <li><a href="/">Home</a></li>
        <li><a href="/about/">About</a></li>
        <li><a href="/contact/">Contact</a></li>
      </ul>
    </nav>
    <main>
      {% block content %}
      {% endblock %}
    </main>
    {% include 'footer.html' %}
</body>
</html>
```

In this example, the `header.html` and `footer.html` templates define the header and footer components, respectively. These components are then included in the `base.html` template using the `{% include %}` template tag, allowing them to be reused across multiple pages.

Best Practices for Creating Reusable Templates and Layouts

1. Keep Templates Simple: Define base templates with minimal logic and focus on layout structure and common elements.

2. Use Template Inheritance Wisely: Break down complex layouts into smaller components and use template inheritance to compose them as needed.

3. Organize Templates: Organize templates into logical directories and use descriptive names to make it easier to navigate and maintain the template structure.

4. Test Layouts Across Pages: Test layout templates across different pages and screen sizes to ensure consistency and responsiveness.

Creating reusable templates and extending layouts is a fundamental practice in Django full-stack development for building modular, maintainable, and scalable web applications. By leveraging Django's template language and template inheritance, developers can efficiently define base templates with common elements and extend them in child templates to create consistent and cohesive user interfaces. With the knowledge and techniques outlined in this guide, you'll be well-equipped to create reusable templates and extend layouts effectively in your Django projects, delivering engaging and user-friendly web experiences.

Integrating User Authentication with Templates in Django

User authentication is a fundamental aspect of web development, ensuring that only authorized users can access certain features or resources within an application. In this guide, we'll explore how to integrate user authentication with templates in a Django full-stack development environment. By leveraging Django's built-in authentication system and template rendering capabilities, we can create secure and user-friendly web applications.

1. Setting Up the Django Project: Install Django: If you haven't already, install Django using pip:

pip install django

- Create a new Django project:

django-admin startproject project_name

- Navigate into the project directory:

```
cd project_name
```

2. Creating a Django App: Create a new Django app within the project:

```
python manage.py startapp app_name
```

3. Configuring User Authentication: Django provides a built-in authentication system, including user models, views, and forms.

- Configure the authentication settings in the project's settings.py file:

```python
# settings.py

INSTALLED_APPS = [
    ...
    'django.contrib.auth',
    'django.contrib.contenttypes',
    'django.contrib.sessions',
    'django.contrib.messages',
    'django.contrib.staticfiles',
]
```

```
```

Run migrations to create the necessary database tables for authentication:

```
python manage.py makemigrations
python manage.py migrate
```

4. Creating User Registration and Login Templates:

Create HTML templates for user registration and login forms:

```html
<!-- registration.html -->
<form method="post">
    {% csrf_token %}
    {{ form.as_p }}
    <button type="submit">Register</button>
</form>
```

```html
<!-- login.html -->
<form method="post">
    {% csrf_token %}
    {{ form.as_p }}
    <button type="submit">Login</button>
</form>
```

5. Configuring URL Patterns: Define URL patterns for user registration and login views in the app's urls.py file:

```python
# urls.py

from django.urls import path
from . import views

urlpatterns = [
    path('register/', views.register, name='register'),
    path('login/', views.user_login, name='login'),
]
```

6. Implementing Views for User Authentication:
Create views to handle user registration and login logic in the app's views.py file:

```python
# views.py

from django.shortcuts import render, redirect
from django.contrib.auth.forms import UserCreationForm, AuthenticationForm
from django.contrib.auth import login, authenticate
```

```
def register(request):
    if request.method == 'POST':
        form = UserCreationForm(request.POST)
        if form.is_valid():
            form.save()
            username = form.cleaned_data.get('username')
            raw_password =
form.cleaned_data.get('password1')
            user = authenticate(username=username,
password=raw_password)
            login(request, user)
            return redirect('home')
    else:
        form = UserCreationForm()
    return render(request, 'registration.html', {'form':
form})

def user_login(request):
    if request.method == 'POST':
        form = AuthenticationForm(request,
data=request.POST)
        if form.is_valid():
            username = form.cleaned_data.get('username')
            password = form.cleaned_data.get('password')
            user = authenticate(username=username,
password=password)
            if user is not None:
                login(request, user)
```

```
            return redirect('home')
    else:
        form = AuthenticationForm()
    return render(request, 'login.html', {'form': form})
```

7. Protecting Views with Authentication: To restrict access to certain views to authenticated users, use the `login_required` decorator:

```python
from django.contrib.auth.decorators import login_required

@login_required
def my_protected_view(request):
    # View logic here
```

Integrating user authentication with templates in Django is essential for creating secure web applications. By following the steps outlined in this guide, you can implement user registration, login, and access control features efficiently. Django's built-in authentication system provides robust functionality while templates allow for flexible and customizable user interfaces.

Securing Your Templates with Context Processors in Django

In Django web development, ensuring the security of your templates is crucial to protect sensitive data and prevent vulnerabilities such as cross-site scripting (XSS) attacks. Context processors play a vital role in enhancing template security by providing additional context variables to all templates across your Django project. In this guide, we'll explore how to secure your templates using context processors in a Django full-stack development environment.

1. Understanding Context Processors:

- Context processors in Django are Python functions that add data to the context of all templates.

- These functions run before the template is rendered and can dynamically add variables to the template context.

- Context processors are defined in Python modules and configured in the Django settings.

2. Creating a Context Processor:

- To create a context processor, define a Python function that returns a dictionary of context variables.

- Context processors should be placed in a suitable location within your Django project.

Here's an example of a context processor that adds a variable indicating whether the current user is authenticated:

```python
# myapp/context_processors.py

def auth_status(request):
    return {
        'user_authenticated':
request.user.is_authenticated
    }
```

3. Configuring Context Processors:

- Once you've created your context processor functions, you need to configure them in the Django settings.

- Add the path to your context processors in the `TEMPLATES` setting under the `OPTIONS` key:

```python
# settings.py

TEMPLATES = [
    {
        'OPTIONS': {
            'context_processors': [

                'myapp.context_processors.auth_status',
```

4. Using Context Variables in Templates:

- Once configured, the context variables provided by context processors are available in all templates.

- You can access these variables directly within your template files.

For example, to display content based on the authentication status of the user:

```html
```

```
<!-- base.html -->

{% if user_authenticated %}
  <p>Welcome, {{ request.user.username }}!</p>
  <a href="{% url 'logout' %}">Logout</a>
{% else %}
  <a href="{% url 'login' %}">Login</a>
{% endif %}
```

5. Enhancing Template Security: Context processors can be used to enhance template security by providing additional context variables related to security features.

For example, you can include a CSRF token in all templates to prevent CSRF attacks:

```python
# myapp/context_processors.py

from django.middleware.csrf import get_token

def csrf_token(request):
    return {
        'csrf_token': get_token(request)
    }
```

6. Implementing Content Security Policy (CSP):

- Content Security Policy (CSP) is a security standard that helps prevent XSS attacks by specifying approved sources for content.

- You can use a context processor to include CSP directives in all templates:

```python
# myapp/context_processors.py

def content_security_policy(request):
    return {
        'content_security_policy': {
            'default-src': ["'self'"],
            'script-src': ["'self'",
"https://cdnjs.cloudflare.com"],
            'style-src': ["'self'",
"https://stackpath.bootstrapcdn.com"],
```

7. Testing Template Security:

- After implementing context processors for template security, it's essential to thoroughly test your application.

- Test for vulnerabilities such as XSS by attempting to inject malicious scripts into form inputs and other user-generated content.

- Use security scanning tools and perform regular security audits to identify and mitigate potential risks.

Securing your templates with context processors in Django is an effective way to enhance the security of your web application. By dynamically adding context variables to all templates, context processors enable you to implement security features such as authentication status indicators, CSRF token inclusion, and Content Security Policy directives. By following the steps outlined in this guide, you can ensure that your Django project is protected against common web security threats.

Chapter 11

Choosing the Right Local Development Environment for Django Full Stack Development

Selecting the appropriate local development environment is crucial for efficient and seamless Django full-stack development. A well-chosen environment can enhance productivity, facilitate collaboration, and streamline the development process. In this guide, we'll explore different options for local development environments tailored specifically for Django projects, along with their pros and cons.

1. Native Environment Setup:

- Setting up a native development environment involves installing Django and its dependencies directly on your local machine.

- This approach offers maximum control and flexibility, allowing you to customize your development setup according to your specific requirements.

To set up a native environment, follow these steps:

```
pip install django

django-admin startproject project_name
```

Pros:

- Full control over dependencies and configurations.

- Direct access to system resources for optimal performance.

- Seamless integration with local development tools and workflows.

Cons:

- Dependency management can become complex, especially for projects with multiple dependencies.

- Environment setup may vary across different machines, leading to inconsistencies.

- Potential conflicts with existing system configurations or dependencies.

2. Virtual Environments:

- Virtual environments provide isolated Python environments for individual projects, allowing you to manage dependencies independently.

- Tools like virtualenv and venv are commonly used to create and manage virtual environments.

To set up a virtual environment for your Django project:

pip install virtualenv

virtualenv env

source env/bin/activate

pip install django

Pros:

- Isolated environments prevent dependency conflicts between projects.

- Simplifies dependency management by encapsulating project-specific dependencies.

- Easy to share and reproduce development environments across different machines.

Cons:

- Requires additional setup steps compared to a native environment.

- May result in larger project directories due to the inclusion of virtual environment files.

- Limited access to system resources compared to a native setup.

3. Dockerized Development:

- Docker provides a platform for containerized development environments, allowing you to package your Django application and its dependencies into portable containers.

- Docker Compose simplifies the management of multi-container applications by defining them in a single YAML file.

To set up a Dockerized development environment for Django:

- Create a Dockerfile to define the application's environment and dependencies.

- Create a docker-compose.yml file to orchestrate the application's containers.

- Build and run the Docker containers using Docker Compose commands.

Pros:

- Consistent development environment across different machines and platforms.

- Simplifies collaboration by standardizing the development environment.

- Scalable and efficient resource utilization through containerization.

Cons:

- Requires familiarity with Docker and containerization concepts.

- Overhead of managing Docker images and containers.

- Potential performance overhead compared to native or virtual environments.

4. Integrated Development Environments (IDEs):

- IDEs provide comprehensive development environments with features such as code editors, debugging tools, and project management capabilities.

- Popular IDEs for Django development include PyCharm, Visual Studio Code (with Python extension), and Sublime Text.

To set up an IDE for Django development:

- Install the IDE of your choice.

- Configure project settings, including interpreter paths and project structure.

- Install any necessary extensions or plugins for Django development.

Pros:

- Rich set of features tailored for Django development, including code completion, debugging, and version control integration.

- Streamlined workflow with integrated tools for testing, profiling, and deployment.

- Active community support and extensive documentation for popular IDEs.

Cons:

- Learning curve associated with mastering the features and workflows of the IDE.

- Resource-intensive compared to lightweight text editors.

- License fees may apply for certain IDEs or advanced features.

5. Lightweight Text Editors:

- Lightweight text editors offer simplicity and versatility for Django development, with minimal overhead and resource consumption.

- Editors like Sublime Text, Atom, and Visual Studio Code are popular choices among developers.

To set up a lightweight text editor for Django development:

- Install the text editor of your choice.

- Install relevant extensions or plugins for Python and Django development.

- Configure project settings and preferences according to your preferences.

<u>**Pros**</u>:

- Lightweight and fast performance, ideal for developers who prefer minimalistic environments.

- Extensibility through plugins and extensions, allowing customization based on specific requirements.

- Wide range of available text editors, catering to diverse preferences and workflows.

<u>**Cons**</u>:

- Lack of built-in features compared to full-fledged IDEs.

- Limited support for advanced development tasks such as debugging and profiling.

- May require additional setup for integrating with external tools and services.

Choosing the right local development environment is essential for maximizing productivity and efficiency in Django full-stack development. Whether you opt for a native setup, virtual environments, Dockerized development, IDEs, or lightweight text editors, each approach offers unique advantages and considerations. By evaluating your project requirements, preferences, and team collaboration needs, you can select the most suitable environment to support your Django development workflow effectively.

Installing Python, Django, and Other Dependencies

To install Python, Django, and other dependencies for Django full-stack development, you'll need to follow a few steps. Let's break it down:

Step 1: Install Python

First, you need to install Python. You can download the latest version from the [official Python website](https://www.python.org/downloads/) or use a package manager like Homebrew (for macOS/Linux) or Chocolatey (for Windows).

For macOS/Linux:
```bash
brew install python
```

For Windows:
```bash
choco install python
```

Step 2: Install Django

Once Python is installed, you can install Django using pip, Python's package installer.

```bash
pip install django
```

This will install the latest version of Django.

Step 3: Set Up a Virtual Environment

It's a good practice to work within a virtual environment to manage dependencies for different projects.

```bash
# Create a virtual environment
python -m venv myenv

# Activate the virtual environment
# For macOS/Linux:
source myenv/bin/activate

# For Windows:
myenv\Scripts\activate
```

Step 4: Create a Django Project

Now, you can create a new Django project.

```bash
django-admin startproject myproject
```

This will create a directory called `myproject` with the initial Django project structure.

Step 5: Install Other Dependencies

Depending on your project's requirements, you may need to install additional dependencies. You can do this using pip and a `requirements.txt` file.

Create a `requirements.txt` file and add your dependencies:

```txt
django-environ
django-crispy-forms
django-bootstrap4
```

Then, install the dependencies:

```bash
pip install -r requirements.txt
```

Step 6: Set Up Database

Configure your database settings in the `settings.py` file within your Django project directory. Django supports various databases, including SQLite, PostgreSQL, MySQL, and Oracle.

```python
```

```python
# settings.py

DATABASES = {
    'default': {
        'ENGINE': 'django.db.backends.sqlite3',
        'NAME': BASE_DIR / 'db.sqlite3',
    }
}
```

Step 7: Migrate Database

Once your database settings are configured, you need to create the database schema.

```bash
python manage.py migrate
```

This command will create necessary database tables based on your Django models.

Step 8: Run the Development Server

You can now run the Django development server to see your project in action.

```bash
python manage.py runserver
```

```
```

Visit `http://127.0.0.1:8000/` in your web browser to view your Django project.

In this guide, we've covered the installation of Python, Django, and other dependencies, setting up a virtual environment, creating a Django project, installing additional dependencies, configuring the database, and running the development server. With these steps completed, you're ready to start developing your Django web application!

Configuring Virtual Environments

Configuring virtual environments is crucial for Django full-stack development as it helps manage dependencies and ensures project isolation. Let's delve into setting up and configuring virtual environments for Django projects:

What is a Virtual Environment?

A virtual environment is a self-contained directory tree that contains a Python installation for a particular version of Python, plus a number of additional packages. It allows you to work on a specific project without affecting other projects or the system's Python installation.

Step 1: Install Virtual Environment

If you haven't already installed the `virtualenv` package, you can do so using pip:

```bash
pip install virtualenv
```

Step 2: Create a Virtual Environment

Navigate to your project directory and create a virtual environment:

```bash
cd myproject
virtualenv venv
```

This will create a directory named `venv` which contains a Python interpreter and other necessary files.

Step 3: Activate the Virtual Environment

You need to activate the virtual environment to start using it:

For macOS/Linux:
```bash
source venv/bin/activate
```

For Windows:
```bash
venv\Scripts\activate
```

Step 4: Install Django and Dependencies

With the virtual environment activated, you can now install Django and any other dependencies your project requires. Let's install Django:

```bash
pip install django
```

Step 5: Verify Installation

You can verify that Django is installed correctly by running:

```bash
python -m django --version
```

Step 6: Create a Django Project

Now, you can create a new Django project within your virtual environment:

```bash
django-admin startproject myproject
```

Step 7: Deactivate the Virtual Environment

Once you're done working on your project, you can deactivate the virtual environment:

```bash
deactivate
```

Automating Environment Setup with Pipenv

Alternatively, you can use `pipenv`, a higher-level tool that aims to bring the best of all packaging worlds (bundled with virtualenv, pip, and a few others) to the Python world.

Step 1: Install Pipenv

You can install Pipenv using pip:

```bash
pip install pipenv
```

Step 2: Create a New Project and Virtual Environment

Navigate to your project directory and create a new Pipenv environment:

```bash
cd myproject
pipenv install django
```

This will create a new virtual environment and install Django.

Step 3: Activate the Pipenv Shell

You can activate the Pipenv shell to start working within the virtual environment:

```bash
pipenv shell
```

Step 4: Verify Installation

You can verify that Django is installed correctly by running:

```bash
python -m django --version
```

Step 5: Create a Django Project

Now, you can create a new Django project within your virtual environment:

```bash
django-admin startproject myproject
```

Step 6: Deactivate the Pipenv Shell

Once you're done working on your project, you can exit the Pipenv shell:

```bash
exit
```

In this guide, we've covered the process of setting up and configuring virtual environments for Django full-stack development using both `virtualenv` and `pipenv`. Virtual environments are essential for managing dependencies and ensuring project isolation, allowing developers to work on multiple projects with different dependencies without conflicts. By following these steps, you can create and manage virtual environments for your Django projects effectively.

Working with Databases Locally

Working with databases locally is a fundamental aspect of Django full-stack development. Django provides robust support for various databases, including SQLite (which is included by default), PostgreSQL, MySQL, and Oracle. Let's explore how to work with databases locally in a Django project:

Step 1: Configure Database Settings

Django projects come with a default configuration for SQLite in the `settings.py` file. However, you can easily switch to other databases by configuring the `DATABASES` setting. For example, to use PostgreSQL, you would configure it like this:

```python
# settings.py
```

```
DATABASES = {
    'default': {
        'ENGINE': 'django.db.backends.postgresql',
        'NAME': 'mydatabase',
        'USER': 'myuser',
        'PASSWORD': 'mypassword',
        'HOST': 'localhost',
        'PORT': '5432',
    }
```
```

## Step 2: Install Database Driver

Depending on the database you choose, you may need to install the appropriate Python database driver. For PostgreSQL, you would typically use `psycopg2`.

```bash
pip install psycopg2
```

Step 3: Create Database (if necessary)

For SQLite, Django will create the database file automatically when needed. However, for other databases like PostgreSQL or MySQL, you may need to create the database manually.
```

For PostgreSQL:

```bash
createdb mydatabase
```

Step 4: Run Migrations

Once the database is configured, you need to run migrations to create necessary tables and schema for your Django models.

```bash
python manage.py migrate
```

Step 5: Create Superuser (optional)

If your project requires user authentication, you can create a superuser to access the Django admin interface.

```bash
python manage.py createsuperuser
```

Step 6: Interact with the Database

You can interact with the database using Django's built-in ORM (Object-Relational Mapping) system. For example, you can create, read, update, and delete records using Django models.

```python
# models.py

from django.db import models

class MyModel(models.Model):
    name = models.CharField(max_length=100)
    email = models.EmailField()
```

Step 7: Querying Data

You can query data from the database using Django's queryset API.

```python
# views.py

from django.shortcuts import render
from .models import MyModel

def my_view(request):
    data = MyModel.objects.all()
```

```
    return render(request, 'my_template.html', {'data':
data})
```

Step 8: Django Admin Interface

Django comes with a built-in admin interface that allows
you to perform CRUD operations on your models.

```python
# admin.py

from django.contrib import admin
from .models import MyModel

admin.site.register(MyModel)
```

Step 9: Run Development Server

You can now run the development server and start
interacting with your Django project locally.

```bash
python manage.py runserver
```

In this guide, we've covered the process of working with databases locally in a Django full-stack development environment. We configured database settings, installed database drivers, created databases, ran migrations, interacted with the database using Django's ORM, and explored the Django admin interface. By following these steps, you can effectively manage and interact with databases in your Django projects, allowing for efficient development and testing locally before deploying to production environments.

Chapter 12

Understanding Different Deployment Options (Cloud, Shared Hosting)

Understanding different deployment options for Django full-stack development is crucial for deploying your projects to production environments. Let's explore two common deployment options: deploying to the cloud and shared hosting.

Cloud Deployment

Cloud deployment involves hosting your Django application on cloud platforms such as AWS, Google Cloud Platform (GCP), Microsoft Azure, or Heroku. These platforms offer scalability, reliability, and various services to support deploying web applications.

Step 1: Set Up Cloud Account

Sign up for an account on your preferred cloud platform and create a new project.

Step 2: Configure Database

Choose a database service provided by the cloud platform, such as Amazon RDS for AWS or Google

Cloud SQL for GCP. Configure your Django application to use the cloud database.

```python
# settings.py

DATABASES = {
    'default': {
        'ENGINE': 'django.db.backends.postgresql',
        'NAME': 'mydatabase',
        'USER': 'myuser',
        'PASSWORD': 'mypassword',
        'HOST': 'mydatabaseinstance.xxxxxx.us-west-2.rds.amazonaws.com',
        'PORT': '5432',
    }
```

Step 3: Static and Media Files

Configure static and media file storage using cloud storage services like Amazon S3 or Google Cloud Storage.

```python
# settings.py

AWS_ACCESS_KEY_ID = 'your-access-key'
```

```
AWS_SECRET_ACCESS_KEY = 'your-secret-key'
AWS_STORAGE_BUCKET_NAME = 'your-bucket-
name'

DEFAULT_FILE_STORAGE =
'storages.backends.s3boto3.S3Boto3Storage'
STATICFILES_STORAGE =
'storages.backends.s3boto3.S3Boto3Storage'
```

Step 4: Deploy to Platform

Deploy your Django application to the cloud platform
using tools like AWS Elastic Beanstalk, Google App
Engine, Azure App Service, or Heroku.

```bash
git push heroku master
```

Step 5: Scale as Needed

Cloud platforms offer scalability features that allow you
to scale your application horizontally or vertically based
on demand.

<u>**Shared Hosting**</u>

Shared hosting involves hosting your Django application on a server shared with other users. While it's usually less expensive, it may have limitations in terms of performance and scalability compared to cloud hosting.

Step 1: Choose a Hosting Provider

Select a shared hosting provider that supports Django applications. Some popular options include Bluehost, HostGator, and SiteGround.

Step 2: Set Up Hosting Account

Sign up for a hosting account and configure your domain name.

Step 3: Configure Server Environment

Access your server using SSH and configure the server environment. Install necessary dependencies such as Python, Django, and a web server like Apache or Nginx.

```bash
sudo apt-get update
sudo apt-get install python3 python3-pip nginx
```

Step 4: Configure Django Application

Upload your Django application to the server and configure the web server to serve your application.

```nginx
# /etc/nginx/sites-available/myproject

server {
    listen 80;
    server_name example.com;

    location = /favicon.ico { access_log off;
log_not_found off; }
    location /static/ {
        root /path/to/static/files;
    }
    location / {
        include proxy_params;
        proxy_pass
http://unix:/path/to/socket/myproject.sock;
    }
```

Step 5: Deploy Django Application

Deploy your Django application using tools like Git or FTP to upload files to the server.

```bash
python manage.py collectstatic
```

Step 6: Set Up Database

Set up a database for your Django application. Many
shared hosting providers offer MySQL or PostgreSQL
databases.

Step 7: Configure Settings

Update your Django settings to use the shared hosting
database and configure static and media file paths
accordingly.

```python
# settings.py

DATABASES = {
    'default': {
        'ENGINE': 'django.db.backends.mysql',
        'NAME': 'mydatabase',
        'USER': 'myuser',
        'PASSWORD': 'mypassword',
        'HOST': 'localhost',
        'PORT': '3306',
    }
```

```
STATIC_URL = '/static/'
STATIC_ROOT = '/path/to/static/files/'
MEDIA_URL = '/media/'
MEDIA_ROOT = '/path/to/media/files/'
```

Step 8: Set Up Email (if needed)

Configure email settings for your Django application, such as SMTP settings or using third-party email services.

Step 9: Test and Monitor

Test your Django application on the shared hosting environment and monitor performance. Consider optimizing performance using caching, compression, and other techniques.

In this guide, we've explored different deployment options for Django full-stack development: cloud deployment and shared hosting. Cloud deployment offers scalability and reliability but may be more complex and expensive. Shared hosting is cost-effective and straightforward but may have limitations in terms of performance and scalability. By understanding these deployment options and following the steps outlined, you can choose the best deployment strategy for your Django projects based on your requirements and budget.

Configuring Web Servers for Django Applications

Configuring web servers for Django applications is essential for serving your application to users over the internet. Two popular choices for web servers are Apache and Nginx. Let's explore how to configure both for Django full-stack development:

Apache Configuration

Apache is a widely used web server with support for various platforms and technologies. Here's how to configure Apache for serving Django applications:

Step 1: Install Apache and Mod_WSGI

```bash
sudo apt-get update
sudo apt-get install apache2 libapache2-mod-wsgi-py3
```

Step 2: Configure Virtual Host

Create a virtual host configuration file for your Django application:

```bash
sudo nano /etc/apache2/sites-available/myproject.conf
```

Add the following configuration:

```apache
<VirtualHost *:80>
    ServerName example.com
    ServerAlias www.example.com

    DocumentRoot /path/to/myproject

    <Directory /path/to/myproject>
      <Files wsgi.py>
        Require all granted
      </Files>
    </Directory>

    WSGIDaemonProcess myproject python-path=/path/to/myproject:/path/to/venv/lib/python3.x/site-packages
    WSGIProcessGroup myproject
    WSGIScriptAlias / /path/to/myproject/wsgi.py

    ErrorLog ${APACHE_LOG_DIR}/error.log
    CustomLog ${APACHE_LOG_DIR}/access.log combined
```

```
</VirtualHost>
```

Step 3: Enable Virtual Host

Enable the virtual host configuration and restart Apache:

```bash
sudo a2ensite myproject.conf
sudo systemctl restart apache2
```

Step 4: Configure Django Settings

Update your Django settings to allow the Apache server to serve your application:

```python
# settings.py

ALLOWED_HOSTS = ['example.com',
'www.example.com']
```

<u>Nginx Configuration</u>

Nginx is a high-performance web server known for its scalability and efficiency. Here's how to configure Nginx for serving Django applications:

Step 1: Install Nginx and uWSGI

```bash
sudo apt-get update
sudo apt-get install nginx uwsgi uwsgi-plugin-python3
```

Step 2: Configure Nginx

Create a server block configuration file for your Django application:

```bash
sudo nano /etc/nginx/sites-available/myproject
```

Add the following configuration:

```nginx
server {
    listen 80;
    server_name example.com www.example.com;

    location = /favicon.ico { access_log off;
log_not_found off; }
    location /static/ {
```

```
      root /path/to/myproject;
   }
   location /media/ {
      root /path/to/myproject;
   }
   location / {
      include uwsgi_params;
      uwsgi_pass
unix:/path/to/myproject/myproject.sock;
   }
```

Step 3: Enable Nginx Server Block

Create a symbolic link to enable the server block
configuration and restart Nginx:

```bash
sudo ln -s /etc/nginx/sites-available/myproject
/etc/nginx/sites-enabled
sudo systemctl restart nginx
```

Step 4: Configure uWSGI

Create a uWSGI configuration file for your Django
application:

```bash
sudo nano /etc/uwsgi/apps-available/myproject.ini
```

Add the following configuration:

```ini
[uwsgi]
chdir = /path/to/myproject
module = myproject.wsgi:application
uid = www-data
gid = www-data
socket = /path/to/myproject/myproject.sock
chmod-socket = 660
vacuum = true
```

Step 5: Enable uWSGI Configuration

Create a symbolic link to enable the uWSGI configuration and restart uWSGI:

```bash
sudo ln -s /etc/uwsgi/apps-available/myproject.ini /etc/uwsgi/apps-enabled
sudo systemctl restart uwsgi
```

Step 6: Configure Django Settings

Update your Django settings to allow Nginx and uWSGI to serve your application:

```python
# settings.py

ALLOWED_HOSTS = ['example.com',
'www.example.com']
```

In this guide, we've explored how to configure Apache and Nginx web servers for serving Django applications. Both servers offer reliable performance and scalability, and the choice between them depends on your specific requirements and preferences. By following the steps outlined above and configuring your web server correctly, you can deploy your Django application and serve it to users over the internet with ease.

Managing Static Files and Media Uploads

Managing static files and media uploads is an essential aspect of Django full-stack development. Static files include CSS, JavaScript, images, and other assets used to style and enhance the user interface of your web application. Media files, on the other hand, include user-uploaded content such as images, videos, and documents. Let's explore how to manage static files and media uploads in Django:

Static Files

Django provides a built-in mechanism for managing static files using the `STATICFILES_DIRS` and `STATIC_ROOT` settings in the `settings.py` file.

Step 1: Define Static Files Directory

First, define the directory where your static files are located. By default, Django looks for static files in the `static` directory within each app. You can also define additional directories using the `STATICFILES_DIRS` setting.

```python
# settings.py

STATICFILES_DIRS = [
    '/path/to/static/files/',
    '/path/to/another/static/directory/',
]
```

Step 2: Collect Static Files

Before deploying your application, you need to collect all static files into a single directory. Django provides a management command for this purpose:

```bash
python manage.py collectstatic
```

This command will copy all static files from each app's `static` directory and additional directories defined in `STATICFILES_DIRS` to a single directory specified by `STATIC_ROOT`.

Step 3: Serve Static Files

In development, Django automatically serves static files using the `django.contrib.staticfiles` app. However, in production, you need to configure your web server to serve static files directly. For example, with Nginx:

```nginx
server {

    location /static/ {
        alias /path/to/static/files/;
    }
```

Media Uploads

Media uploads refer to files uploaded by users through your web application, such as profile pictures, documents, or multimedia content. Django provides a built-in `FileField` and `ImageField` for handling media uploads.

Step 1: Define Media Uploads Directory

Define the directory where media files will be uploaded. You can use the `MEDIA_ROOT` setting in `settings.py` to specify the directory:

```python
# settings.py

MEDIA_ROOT = '/path/to/media/uploads/'
```

Step 2: Define Media URL

Define the URL prefix for serving media files. You can use the `MEDIA_URL` setting in `settings.py`:

```python
# settings.py
```

MEDIA_URL = '/media/'
```

## Step 3: Handle File Uploads in Models

In your Django models, use `FileField` or `ImageField` to handle file uploads:

```python
# models.py

from django.db import models

class UserProfile(models.Model):
    username = models.CharField(max_length=100)
    profile_picture =
models.ImageField(upload_to='profile_pictures/')
```

Step 4: Configure URL Patterns

In your Django project's `urls.py`, configure URL patterns to serve media files during development:

```python
# urls.py

from django.conf import settings
```
```

```python
from django.conf.urls.static import static
from django.urls import path

urlpatterns = [

] + static(settings.MEDIA_URL,
document_root=settings.MEDIA_ROOT)
```

Step 5: Handle File Uploads in Views

In your Django views, handle file uploads using Django forms:

```python
# views.py

from django.shortcuts import render
from .forms import UserProfileForm

def upload_profile_picture(request):
    if request.method == 'POST':
        form = UserProfileForm(request.POST,
request.FILES)
        if form.is_valid():
            form.save()
            return redirect('profile')
    else:
```

```
    form = UserProfileForm()
  return render(request, 'upload_profile_picture.html',
{'form': form})
```

Step 6: Display Uploaded Files in Templates

In your Django templates, display uploaded files using
appropriate HTML tags:

```html
<!-- upload_profile_picture.html -->

<form method="post" enctype="multipart/form-data">
  {% csrf_token %}
  {{ form.as_p }}
  <button type="submit">Upload</button>
</form>
```

In this guide, we've explored how to manage static files
and media uploads in Django full-stack development.
Static files are managed using the
`STATICFILES_DIRS` and `STATIC_ROOT` settings,
while media uploads are handled using
`MEDIA_ROOT` and `MEDIA_URL`. By following the
steps outlined above, you can effectively manage and

serve static files and media uploads in your Django projects, providing a rich and interactive user experience.

Setting Up Database Connections on the Server

Setting up database connections on the server is a crucial step in deploying Django applications. Whether you're using PostgreSQL, MySQL, SQLite, or another database backend, configuring the connection properly ensures that your application can interact with the database seamlessly. Let's explore how to set up database connections for Django full-stack development:

Step 1: Install Database Server

Before setting up database connections, you need to ensure that the appropriate database server is installed on your server. For example, if you're using PostgreSQL, you would install it like this:

```bash
sudo apt-get update
sudo apt-get install postgresql postgresql-contrib
```

Step 2: Create Database and User (if necessary)

If your Django application requires a specific database and user, you need to create them on the database server. For PostgreSQL, you can create a database and user like this:

```bash
sudo -u postgres psql

CREATE DATABASE mydatabase;
CREATE USER myuser WITH PASSWORD 'mypassword';
ALTER ROLE myuser SET client_encoding TO 'utf8';
ALTER ROLE myuser SET default_transaction_isolation TO 'read committed';
ALTER ROLE myuser SET timezone TO 'UTC';
GRANT ALL PRIVILEGES ON DATABASE mydatabase TO myuser;
```

Step 3: Configure Django Settings

Update your Django application's settings to use the database credentials you've created. Modify the `DATABASES` setting in your `settings.py` file:

```python
# settings.py
```

```
DATABASES = {
  'default': {
    'ENGINE': 'django.db.backends.postgresql',
    'NAME': 'mydatabase',
    'USER': 'myuser',
    'PASSWORD': 'mypassword',
    'HOST': 'localhost',
    'PORT': '5432',
  }
}
```

Step 4: Migrate Database Schema

If you're deploying a new Django application or making changes to the database schema, you need to run migrations to apply those changes to the database.

```bash
python manage.py migrate
```

Step 5: Configure Database Firewall and Security

Ensure that your database server is configured securely and that only authorized users and applications can access it. Configure firewall rules and access controls to restrict access to the database server as needed.

Step 6: Test Database Connection

Test the database connection from your Django application to ensure that it's working correctly. You can do this by running your Django application and performing database operations.

```bash
python manage.py runserver
```

Step 7: Monitor Database Performance

Monitor database performance regularly to identify any potential issues or bottlenecks. Use tools like pgAdmin (for PostgreSQL), MySQL Workbench (for MySQL), or database monitoring services to track database performance metrics.

Step 8: Backup Database Regularly

Set up regular backups for your database to prevent data loss in case of hardware failure, data corruption, or other disasters. Use database backup tools or services to automate the backup process and ensure that backups are stored securely.

Step 9: Scale Database as Needed

As your Django application grows and receives more traffic, you may need to scale your database to handle the increased load. Consider strategies such as vertical scaling (upgrading server hardware) or horizontal scaling (adding more database servers) to improve database performance and scalability.

Step 10: Handle Database Errors Gracefully

Implement error handling mechanisms in your Django application to handle database errors gracefully. Use try-except blocks or Django's built-in error handling features to catch database-related exceptions and provide informative error messages to users.

In this guide, we've covered the process of setting up database connections on the server for Django full-stack development. By following these steps and configuring database settings, migrating database schema, securing the database server, testing the database connection, monitoring performance, backing up the database regularly, scaling the database as needed, and handling database errors gracefully, you can ensure that your Django application interacts with the database effectively and efficiently in a production environment.

Best Practices for Secure Deployment

Securing your Django deployment is crucial to protect your application and its data from unauthorized access, data breaches, and other security threats. By following best practices for secure deployment, you can minimize vulnerabilities and ensure that your Django application is robust and resilient. Let's explore some of the best practices for securing Django deployments:

1. Use HTTPS for Secure Communication

Ensure that all communication between the client and server is encrypted using HTTPS. This prevents eavesdropping, tampering, and man-in-the-middle attacks. You can enable HTTPS by obtaining an SSL/TLS certificate and configuring your web server to use HTTPS.

```nginx
server {
    listen 443 ssl;
    server_name example.com;

    ssl_certificate /path/to/ssl/certificate.crt;
    ssl_certificate_key /path/to/ssl/private.key;
}
```

2. Keep Django and Dependencies Updated

Regularly update Django and its dependencies to the latest versions to patch security vulnerabilities and ensure that your application is protected against known exploits.

```bash
pip install --upgrade django
```

3. Use Strong Passwords and Authentication

Use strong and unique passwords for database credentials, admin accounts, and user accounts. Implement secure authentication mechanisms such as multi-factor authentication (MFA) to add an extra layer of security.

```python
# settings.py

PASSWORD_HASHERS = [
    'django.contrib.auth.hashers.Argon2PasswordHasher',

'django.contrib.auth.hashers.PBKDF2PasswordHasher',
```

]
```

## 4. Secure Database Configuration

Ensure that database credentials are stored securely and not exposed in version control or configuration files. Use environment variables or a secure secrets management system to store sensitive information.

```python
# settings.py

import os

DATABASES = {
    'default': {
        'ENGINE': 'django.db.backends.postgresql',
        'NAME': os.environ.get('DB_NAME'),
        'USER': os.environ.get('DB_USER'),
        'PASSWORD': os.environ.get('DB_PASSWORD'),
        'HOST': os.environ.get('DB_HOST'),
        'PORT': os.environ.get('DB_PORT', '5432'),
    }
}
```

5. Implement CSRF Protection
```

Enable Cross-Site Request Forgery (CSRF) protection to prevent attackers from exploiting user sessions to perform unauthorized actions on behalf of users.

```python
# settings.py

CSRF_COOKIE_SECURE = True
```

6. Enable Clickjacking Protection

Enable X-Frame-Options header to prevent clickjacking attacks by ensuring that your web pages cannot be embedded within frames on other sites.

```python
# settings.py

X_FRAME_OPTIONS = 'DENY'
```

7. Secure Session Configuration

Ensure that session cookies are transmitted securely over HTTPS and are not accessible to JavaScript to prevent session hijacking attacks.

```python
# settings.py

SESSION_COOKIE_SECURE = True
SESSION_COOKIE_HTTPONLY = True
```

8. Protect Against SQL Injection

Use Django's ORM and query parameterization to protect against SQL injection attacks by sanitizing user input before executing database queries.

```python
# views.py

from django.db import connection

def my_view(request):
    cursor = connection.cursor()
    cursor.execute("SELECT * FROM my_table WHERE id = %s", [user_id])
    row = cursor.fetchone()
```

9. Implement Rate Limiting

Implement rate limiting to prevent brute force attacks and Denial of Service (DoS) attacks by limiting the number of requests that a user can make within a certain time period.

```python
# settings.py

REST_FRAMEWORK = {
    'DEFAULT_THROTTLE_CLASSES': (
        'rest_framework.throttling.AnonRateThrottle',
        'rest_framework.throttling.UserRateThrottle',
    ),
    'DEFAULT_THROTTLE_RATES': {
        'anon': '100/day',
        'user': '1000/day',
    }
```

10. Regular Security Audits and Penetration Testing

Perform regular security audits and penetration testing to identify and address security vulnerabilities in your Django application. Use automated tools and manual testing techniques to assess the security posture of your application.

In this guide, we've covered some of the best practices for securing Django deployments. By following these best practices, you can enhance the security of your Django application and protect it against various security threats. Remember to keep Django and its dependencies updated, use HTTPS for secure communication, implement strong authentication and access controls, and regularly audit and test your application for security vulnerabilities. By prioritizing security throughout the development and deployment process, you can build and maintain a secure and robust Django application.

Chapter 13

Pro Tips and Best Practices for Django Development

Streamlining Your Workflow with Shortcuts and Tools

In the dynamic world of web development, optimizing your workflow is crucial for productivity and success. With Django, a powerful Python web framework, developers can build full stack web applications efficiently. However, even with Django's robust features, there are numerous opportunities to streamline the development process further. In this guide, we'll explore essential shortcuts and tools tailored for Django full stack development, empowering developers to work smarter and faster.

Setting Up Your Development Environment

A well-configured development environment is the foundation for efficient Django development. Let's start by creating a virtual environment and installing Django using `pip`.

```bash
# Create a virtual environment
python3 -m venv myenv
```

```
# Activate the virtual environment
source myenv/bin/activate

# Install Django
pip install django
```

Utilizing Django Extensions

Django Extensions is a collection of custom extensions
for Django projects, providing additional management
commands and utilities. Install Django Extensions using
`pip`.

```bash
# Install Django Extensions
pip install django-extensions
```

With Django Extensions, you gain access to various
shortcuts and tools to streamline your development
process.

Generating Django Apps Quickly

Django's `startapp` command allows you to create new
Django apps. However, Django Extensions offers an

enhanced version of this command with additional
features.

```bash
# Generate a new Django app with Django Extensions
python manage.py generate_app myapp
```

This command creates a new Django app with default
directory structure and files, saving you time and effort.

Database Management Made Easy

Django Extensions simplifies database management
tasks with its `reset_db` and `reset_schema` commands.

```bash
# Reset the database
python manage.py reset_db

# Reset database schema
python manage.py reset_schema
```

These commands streamline the process of resetting the
database or schema during development.

Interactive Shell Plus

Django's default shell (`python manage.py shell`) is useful for interacting with your application's models and database. However, Django Extensions provides an enhanced shell with auto-imports and history support.

```bash
# Start an enhanced Django shell
python manage.py shell_plus
```

The Interactive Shell Plus saves time by automatically importing models and providing a more interactive development experience.

Code Generation with Django Extensions

Django Extensions offers shortcuts for generating boilerplate code, such as model diagrams and admin classes.

```bash
# Generate a graphviz diagram of Django models
python manage.py graph_models -a -o myapp_models.png

# Generate admin classes for Django models
python manage.py generate_admin myapp
```

```
```

These commands accelerate the development process by automating the generation of common code patterns.

Debugging with Django Debug Toolbar

The Django Debug Toolbar is a valuable debugging tool that provides insights into request/response cycles, database queries, and cache usage.

```bash
# Install Django Debug Toolbar
pip install django-debug-toolbar
```

After installation, configure the Debug Toolbar in your Django project's settings.

```python
# settings.py

DEBUG = True

INSTALLED_APPS = [

    'debug_toolbar',
```

MIDDLEWARE = [

'debug_toolbar.middleware.DebugToolbarMiddleware',

```
```

With the Debug Toolbar enabled, you can diagnose performance issues and optimize your application effectively.

Automating Testing with Django Test Runner

Django's built-in test runner simplifies the process of writing and executing tests for your application.

```bash
# Run tests for your Django app
python manage.py test
```

By writing comprehensive tests and running them regularly, you can ensure the reliability and stability of your application.

Version Control with Git

Version control is essential for collaboration and code management in software development. Initialize a Git repository for your Django project and commit your code regularly.

```bash
# Initialize a new Git repository
git init

# Add your project files to the repository
git add .

# Commit the changes
git commit -m "Initial commit"
```

Using Git allows you to track changes, collaborate with team members, and revert to previous versions if needed.

Continuous Integration and Deployment

Automating the deployment process with continuous integration (CI) tools like Jenkins or GitLab CI ensures consistency and reliability in your deployment workflow.

```yaml
# .gitlab-ci.yml

stages:
```

```
  - test
  - deploy

test:
  stage: test
  script:
    - python manage.py test

deploy:
  stage: deploy
  script:
    - ./deploy.sh
```

Configure your CI pipeline to run tests and deploy your application automatically when changes are pushed to the repository.

By leveraging shortcuts and tools tailored for Django full stack development, developers can enhance their workflow and focus on building high-quality web applications. From setting up a well-configured development environment to automating testing and deployment, each tool plays a crucial role in streamlining the development process. By adopting these best practices and utilizing the right tools, developers can improve productivity, reduce errors, and deliver exceptional web applications with Django.

Writing Clean, Maintainable, and Efficient Django Code

In the world of web development, writing clean, maintainable, and efficient code is essential for building successful applications. Django, a high-level Python web framework, provides developers with powerful tools and conventions to write robust web applications. In this guide, we'll explore best practices and coding techniques for writing clean, maintainable, and efficient Django code.

Organizing Your Django Project

A well-organized project structure lays the foundation for clean and maintainable code. Django's recommended project structure separates different components of your application, such as apps, static files, and templates.

```plaintext
myproject/
├── myproject/
│   ├── settings.py
│   ├── urls.py
│   └── wsgi.py
├── myapp1/
│   ├── migrations/
│   ├── templates/
```
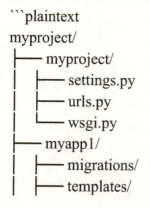

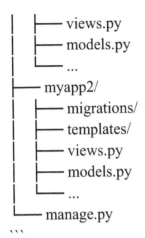

```
|        ├── views.py
|        ├── models.py
|        └── ...
├── myapp2/
|        ├── migrations/
|        ├── templates/
|        ├── views.py
|        ├── models.py
|        └── ...
└── manage.py
```

By organizing your project into distinct apps and modules, you can maintain a clear structure and facilitate collaboration among team members.

Writing Modular and Reusable Code

Django encourages modular and reusable code through the concept of apps. Each app in a Django project should focus on a specific functionality or feature.

```python
# myapp/models.py

from django.db import models

class MyModel(models.Model):
```

```python
name = models.CharField(max_length=100)
description = models.TextField()

def __str__(self):
    return self.name
```

By defining models, views, and templates within individual apps, you can create self-contained components that are easy to understand and maintain.

Following the DRY Principle

The Don't Repeat Yourself (DRY) principle is a fundamental tenet of software development. In Django, you can avoid repetition by leveraging inheritance and reusable components.

```python
# myproject/settings.py

DATABASES = {
    'default': {
        'ENGINE': 'django.db.backends.sqlite3',
        'NAME': 'mydatabase',
    }
```

By defining settings, middleware, and utility functions in a centralized location, you can minimize redundancy and ensure consistency across your project.

Writing Efficient Queries

Efficient database queries are crucial for optimizing the performance of your Django applications. Django's ORM provides a powerful abstraction for interacting with the database while generating efficient SQL queries.

```python
# views.py

from django.shortcuts import render
from .models import MyModel

def my_view(request):
    queryset = MyModel.objects.filter(name__startswith='A')
    return render(request, 'my_template.html', {'objects': queryset})
```

By utilizing queryset methods like `filter()`, `exclude()`, and `annotate()`, you can retrieve the data you need efficiently and minimize database overhead.

Implementing Caching

Caching is an effective strategy for improving the performance of your Django applications by storing frequently accessed data in memory.

```python
# settings.py

CACHES = {
  'default': {
    'BACKEND':
'django.core.cache.backends.memcached.MemcachedCache',
    'LOCATION': '127.0.0.1:11211',
  }
```

By configuring caching backends like Memcached or Redis, you can reduce the response time of your application and alleviate pressure on your database.

Writing Clean and Readable Code

Clean and readable code is essential for maintaining and scaling your Django applications. Follow Python's PEP 8 style guide and adhere to best practices for naming conventions, code structure, and documentation.

```python
# views.py

from django.shortcuts import render
from .models import MyModel

def my_view(request):

    Render a list of objects starting with 'A'.

    queryset =
MyModel.objects.filter(name__startswith='A')
    return render(request, 'my_template.html', {'objects':
queryset})
```

By writing descriptive function and variable names, adding comments and docstrings, and adhering to consistent coding conventions, you can enhance code readability and maintainability.

Testing Your Code

Comprehensive testing is essential for ensuring the reliability and correctness of your Django applications.

Django provides a built-in testing framework for writing unit tests, integration tests, and functional tests.

```python
# tests.py

from django.test import TestCase
from .models import MyModel

class MyModelTestCase(TestCase):
    def test_model_creation(self):
        obj = MyModel.objects.create(name='Test', description='Test description')
        self.assertEqual(obj.name, 'Test')
```

By writing tests for your models, views, forms, and other components, you can catch bugs early and maintain code quality throughout the development process.

Writing clean, maintainable, and efficient Django code is essential for building successful web applications. By following best practices such as organizing your project structure, writing modular and reusable code, optimizing database queries, and adhering to coding conventions, you can create scalable and robust Django applications. Additionally, thorough testing and documentation ensure the reliability and correctness of your codebase. By adopting these principles and techniques, you can elevate your Django development skills and build high-quality web applications that meet the needs of your users.

Debugging Techniques for Identifying and Fixing Errors in Django Full Stack Development

Debugging is an inevitable part of the software development process, and in Django full stack development, it's essential for identifying and fixing errors efficiently. Whether you're troubleshooting issues with views, models, templates, or database queries, having effective debugging techniques at your disposal can streamline the development process and improve code quality. In this guide, we'll explore various debugging techniques and tools tailored for Django full stack development.

Logging

Logging is a fundamental debugging technique that allows developers to record information about the execution of their code. Django provides a built-in logging framework that can be configured to output messages to different destinations, such as the console, files, or email.

```python
# settings.py

LOGGING = {
    'version': 1,
    'handlers': {
        'console': {
            'level': 'DEBUG',
            'class': 'logging.StreamHandler',
        },
    'loggers': {
    'django': {
            'handlers': ['console'],
            'level': 'DEBUG',
            'propagate': True,
    },
```

By adding logging statements strategically throughout your codebase, you can track the flow of execution and capture valuable information about variables, function calls, and error conditions.

```python
# views.py

import logging
```

```python
logger = logging.getLogger(__name__)

def my_view(request):
    logger.debug('Entering my_view function')
    try:
        # Code that may raise an exception
    except Exception as e:
        logger.exception('An error occurred: %s', e)
```

Debugging Toolbar

The Django Debug Toolbar is a powerful debugging tool that provides real-time insights into various aspects of your Django application, including HTTP requests, database queries, template rendering, and cache usage.

```bash
# Install Django Debug Toolbar
pip install django-debug-toolbar
```

After installing the Debug Toolbar, add it to your list of installed apps and middleware in your Django project's settings.

```python
# settings.py
```

```
INSTALLED_APPS = [

'debug_toolbar',

MIDDLEWARE = [

'debug_toolbar.middleware.DebugToolbarMiddleware',
]
```

With the Debug Toolbar enabled, you can inspect the SQL queries generated by your views, identify performance bottlenecks, and troubleshoot issues with template rendering.

Interactive Debugger

Django's built-in interactive debugger, `manage.py runserver`, provides a convenient way to debug your application in real-time. When an exception occurs during execution, Django's development server displays detailed traceback information in the browser, along with an interactive debugging interface.

```python
# views.py
```

```
def my_view(request):
    # Code that may raise an exception
```

If an exception is raised while processing a request, Django's development server will display a detailed traceback in the browser, allowing you to inspect the state of your application at the time of the error.

Django Shell

The Django shell is a powerful tool for interactively exploring your application's models and database. You can start the Django shell using the `manage.py shell` command and execute Python code in the context of your Django project.

```bash
# Start the Django shell
python manage.py shell
```

Once in the shell, you can interact with your models, execute database queries, and test code snippets to diagnose and troubleshoot issues.

```python
# Django shell
```

```
>>> from myapp.models import MyModel
>>> MyModel.objects.all()
<QuerySet [<MyModel: object1>, <MyModel: object2>,
...]>
```

Unit Testing

Writing comprehensive unit tests is an effective way to
identify and prevent errors in your Django application.
Django provides a built-in testing framework for writing
tests for your models, views, forms, and other
components.

```python
# tests.py

from django.test import TestCase
from myapp.models import MyModel

class MyModelTestCase(TestCase):
    def test_something(self):
        # Test code
```

By writing unit tests that cover different aspects of your
application's functionality, you can ensure that your code

behaves as expected and detect regressions early in the development process.

Database Query Debugging

Optimizing database queries is critical for improving the performance of your Django application. Django's ORM provides a variety of tools and techniques for debugging and optimizing database queries.

```python
# views.py

from django.db import connection

def my_view(request):
    queryset = MyModel.objects.all()
    print(connection.queries)
    return render(request, 'my_template.html', {'objects': queryset})
```

By printing the `connection.queries` attribute, you can inspect the SQL queries generated by your views and identify opportunities for optimization, such as adding indexes or reducing the number of queries.

Debugging is an essential skill for Django full stack developers, allowing them to identify and fix errors efficiently throughout the development process. By leveraging logging, debugging tools like the Django Debug Toolbar and interactive debugger, and unit testing, developers can gain valuable insights into their codebase and ensure the reliability and performance of their Django applications. By adopting these debugging techniques and best practices, developers can streamline their workflow, improve code quality, and deliver robust web applications that meet the needs of their users.

Writing Unit Tests for Your Django Applications

Unit testing is a crucial aspect of software development that ensures the reliability and correctness of your codebase. In Django full stack development, writing unit tests helps validate the behavior of your models, views, forms, and other components, reducing the risk of regressions and errors. In this guide, we'll explore best practices and techniques for writing unit tests for your Django applications, covering various aspects of testing your codebase.

Setting Up Your Test Environment

Django provides a built-in testing framework that simplifies the process of writing and executing unit tests. To get started, create a `tests.py` file within your Django app directory and define test classes for your models, views, and other components.

```python
# myapp/tests.py

from django.test import TestCase
from .models import MyModel

class MyModelTestCase(TestCase):
    def setUp(self):
        self.obj = MyModel.objects.create(name='Test', description='Test description')

    def test_model_creation(self):
        self.assertEqual(self.obj.name, 'Test')
```

In this example, we're using Django's `TestCase` class to define a test case for our `MyModel` model. The `setUp` method is used to set up any preconditions required for the test, such as creating database objects.

Testing Models

When writing unit tests for your Django models, focus on testing the behavior of model methods, properties, and attributes. Use assertions to verify that the model behaves as expected under different conditions.

```python
# myapp/tests.py

class MyModelTestCase(TestCase):
    def test_model_str_method(self):
        obj = MyModel.objects.create(name='Test',
description='Test description')
        self.assertEqual(str(obj), 'Test')
```

By testing model methods such as `__str__`, `save`, and custom methods, you can ensure that your models behave correctly and consistently.

Testing Views

Views are the backbone of your Django application, handling incoming HTTP requests and generating HTTP responses. When writing unit tests for your views, focus on testing the response status codes, content, and behavior under different input conditions.

```python
```

```python
# myapp/tests.py

class MyViewTestCase(TestCase):
    def test_view_response(self):
        response = self.client.get('/myapp/')
        self.assertEqual(response.status_code, 200)
        self.assertContains(response, 'Welcome to myapp')
```

By using Django's `Client` class to simulate HTTP requests, you can test the behavior of your views without needing to run a live server.

Testing Forms

Forms play a critical role in Django applications, facilitating data validation and user input processing. When writing unit tests for your forms, focus on testing form validation, field behavior, and error handling.

```python
# myapp/tests.py

from .forms

import unittest
from .forms import MyForm
```

```
class MyFormTestCase(TestCase):
    def test_valid_form(self):
        form_data = {'name': 'Test', 'email':
'test@example.com'}
        form = MyForm(data=form_data)
        self.assertTrue(form.is_valid())

    def test_invalid_form(self):
        form_data = {'name': '', 'email': 'invalid_email'}
        form = MyForm(data=form_data)
        self.assertFalse(form.is_valid())
        self.assertIn('name', form.errors)
        self.assertIn('email', form.errors)
```
```

By testing both valid and invalid form inputs, you can ensure that your forms perform data validation correctly and handle errors gracefully.

## Testing Middleware and Custom Components

In addition to testing models, views, and forms, it's essential to test any custom middleware, template tags, or other custom components in your Django application. Write unit tests to validate the behavior and functionality of these components, ensuring they behave as expected under different conditions.
```

```python
# myapp/tests.py

from django.contrib.auth.middleware import
AuthenticationMiddleware
from django.contrib.sessions.middleware import
SessionMiddleware
from django.http import HttpRequest

class MiddlewareTestCase(TestCase):
    def test_authentication_middleware(self):
        request = HttpRequest()
        middleware = AuthenticationMiddleware()
        middleware.process_request(request)
        self.assertIsNone(request.user)

    def test_session_middleware(self):
        request = HttpRequest()
        middleware = SessionMiddleware()
        middleware.process_request(request)
        self.assertIsNotNone(request.session)
```

By testing custom middleware and components, you can
verify that they integrate seamlessly with Django's
request/response cycle and behave correctly in various
scenarios.

Running Unit Tests

To run your Django unit tests, use the `manage.py test` command in your terminal. Django's test runner will automatically discover and execute all test cases defined in your project.

```bash
# Run unit tests for your Django app
python manage.py test myapp
```

By running your unit tests regularly, you can catch bugs early, ensure code quality, and maintain the reliability of your Django applications.

Writing unit tests for your Django applications is essential for ensuring code reliability, identifying regressions, and maintaining code quality. By following best practices and techniques for testing models, views, forms, and other components, you can build robust and reliable Django applications that meet the needs of your users. Incorporate unit testing into your development workflow from the outset, and you'll reap the benefits of improved code quality and reliability throughout the development lifecycle.

Chapter 14

Understanding Common Web Security Threats in Django Full Stack Development

Web security is a critical aspect of building and maintaining web applications, especially in Django full stack development. As web applications become more sophisticated and interconnected, they also become more vulnerable to various security threats. In this guide, we'll explore common web security threats and how to mitigate them in the context of Django full stack development.

1. Cross-Site Scripting (XSS)

Cross-Site Scripting (XSS) is a prevalent web security vulnerability that allows attackers to inject malicious scripts into web pages viewed by other users. In Django, XSS attacks can occur when user-supplied data is not properly sanitized or escaped in templates.

```python
# views.py

from django.shortcuts import render
```

```
def my_view(request):
    data = request.GET.get('data', '')
    return render(request, 'my_template.html', {'data':
data})
```

```html
<!-- my_template.html -->

<div>{{ data }}</div>
```

To mitigate XSS attacks in Django, always escape user input when rendering templates using the `|safe` filter or the `autoescape` template tag.

```html
<!-- my_template.html -->

<div>{{ data|safe }}</div>
```

2. Cross-Site Request Forgery (CSRF)

Cross-Site Request Forgery (CSRF) is a security vulnerability that allows attackers to execute unauthorized actions on behalf of authenticated users. In Django, CSRF attacks can occur when an attacker tricks a user into submitting a malicious request to a vulnerable website.

To mitigate CSRF attacks in Django, use Django's built-in CSRF protection middleware, which generates and validates unique tokens for each user session.

```python
# settings.py

MIDDLEWARE = [

    'django.middleware.csrf.CsrfViewMiddleware',
```

```html
<!-- my_template.html -->

<form method="post">
    {% csrf_token %}
    <!-- Form fields -->
</form>
```

3. SQL Injection

SQL Injection is a serious security vulnerability that allows attackers to execute arbitrary SQL queries against a database. In Django, SQL Injection attacks can occur when user-supplied data is not properly sanitized or escaped in database queries.

```python
# views.py

from django.db import connection

def my_view(request):
    username = request.GET.get('username', '')
    cursor = connection.cursor()
    cursor.execute(f"SELECT * FROM users WHERE username = '{username}'")
    # Process query results
```

To mitigate SQL Injection attacks in Django, always use parameterized queries or Django's ORM to safely handle user input in database queries.

```python
# views.py

from myapp.models import User

def my_view(request):
    username = request.GET.get('username', '')
    user = User.objects.get(username=username)
```

```
    # Process user data
```

4. Clickjacking

Clickjacking is a security vulnerability that allows
attackers to trick users into clicking on hidden or
disguised elements on a web page. In Django,
Clickjacking attacks can occur when an attacker embeds
a vulnerable site within a frame or iframe on their own
site.

To mitigate Clickjacking attacks in Django, set the `X-Frame-Options` header to `DENY` or `SAMEORIGIN`
to prevent your site from being embedded in frames on
other domains.

```python
# settings.py

X_FRAME_OPTIONS = 'DENY'
```

5. Authentication and Authorization Issues

Authentication and authorization vulnerabilities can lead
to unauthorized access to sensitive data or functionality
within a web application. In Django, common

authentication and authorization issues include weak passwords, insecure session management, and insufficient access controls.

To mitigate authentication and authorization issues in Django, follow best practices for password hashing, session management, and access control.

```python
# settings.py

PASSWORD_HASHERS = [

'django.contrib.auth.hashers.BCryptSHA256PasswordHasher',
```

```python
# views.py

from django.contrib.auth.decorators import login_required

@login_required
def my_secure_view(request):
    # Authorized view logic
```

Understanding common web security threats is essential for building secure and reliable Django web applications. By mitigating vulnerabilities such as XSS, CSRF, SQL Injection, Clickjacking, and authentication issues, you can protect your application and its users from potential security breaches. Always stay informed about the latest security best practices and techniques, and regularly audit your codebase for potential vulnerabilities. By prioritizing security throughout the development lifecycle, you can build robust and trustworthy web applications with Django.

User Authentication and Authorization in Django

User authentication and authorization are essential components of web applications, ensuring that users can securely access and interact with resources. In Django, a robust authentication and authorization system is built-in, providing developers with powerful tools to manage user accounts, permissions, and access control. In this guide, we'll explore how to implement user authentication and authorization in Django, covering registration, login, logout, password management, and permission control.

1. User Registration

User registration allows new users to create accounts and access the application's features. In Django, user registration can be implemented using the built-in `User` model and forms.

```python
# forms.py

from django import forms
from django.contrib.auth.forms import
UserCreationForm
from django.contrib.auth.models import User

class RegistrationForm(UserCreationForm):
    email = forms.EmailField()

    class Meta:
        model = User
        fields = ['username', 'email', 'password1',
'password2']
```

```python
# views.py

from django.shortcuts import render, redirect
from .forms import RegistrationForm

def register(request):
```

```python
    if request.method == 'POST':
        form = RegistrationForm(request.POST)
        if form.is_valid():
            form.save()
            return redirect('login')
    else:
        form = RegistrationForm()
    return render(request, 'registration/register.html',
{'form': form})
```

```html
<!-- register.html -->

<form method="post">
  {% csrf_token %}
  {{ form.as_p }}
  <button type="submit">Register</button>
</form>
```

2. User Login and Logout

User login allows registered users to authenticate and access protected resources, while user logout terminates the user's session and invalidates their authentication credentials.

```python
```

```python
# views.py

from django.contrib.auth import authenticate, login,
logout

def user_login(request):
    if request.method == 'POST':
        username = request.POST['username']
        password = request.POST['password']
        user = authenticate(request, username=username,
password=password)
        if user is not None:
            login(request, user)
            return redirect('home')
    return render(request, 'registration/login.html')

def user_logout(request):
    logout(request)
    return redirect('home')
```

```html
<!-- login.html -->

<form method="post">
  {% csrf_token %}
  <input type="text" name="username"
placeholder="Username">
```

```
  <input type="password" name="password"
placeholder="Password">
  <button type="submit">Login</button>
</form>
```

3. Password Management

Password management allows users to reset their
passwords if they forget them or want to change them.
Django provides built-in views and forms for password
reset and change functionalities.

```python
# urls.py

from django.contrib.auth import views as auth_views

urlpatterns = [

    path('reset_password/',
auth_views.PasswordResetView.as_view(),
name='reset_password'),
    path('reset_password_sent/',
auth_views.PasswordResetDoneView.as_view(),
name='password_reset_done'),
```

```python
    path('reset/<uidb64>/<token>/',
auth_views.PasswordResetConfirmView.as_view(),
name='password_reset_confirm'),
    path('reset_password_complete/',
auth_views.PasswordResetCompleteView.as_view(),
name='password_reset_complete'),
    path('change_password/',
auth_views.PasswordChangeView.as_view(),
name='change_password'),
    path('change_password_done/',
auth_views.PasswordChangeDoneView.as_view(),
name='change_password_done'),
```

```html
<!-- reset_password.html -->

<form method="post">
  {% csrf_token %}
  <input type="email" name="email"
placeholder="Email">
  <button type="submit">Reset Password</button>
</form>
```

4. Authorization and Permission Control

Authorization and permission control allow
administrators to define granular access controls and

permissions for different user roles within the
application. Django provides a flexible and powerful
permission system that can be customized to suit the
needs of your application.

```python
# models.py

from django.contrib.auth.models import User
from django.db import models

class Article(models.Model):
    title = models.CharField(max_length=100)
    content = models.TextField()
    author = models.ForeignKey(User,
on_delete=models.CASCADE)

# views.py

from django.contrib.auth.decorators import
login_required
from django.shortcuts import render
from .models import Article

@login_required
def create_article(request):
    if request.method == 'POST':
        # Process form data and save article
```

```
    return render(request, 'create_article.html')
```
```

In this example, the `create_article` view is decorated with `@login_required`, ensuring that only authenticated users can access it. Additionally, you can implement custom permission checks and role-based access control (RBAC) using Django's built-in `@permission_required` and `@user_passes_test` decorators.

User authentication and authorization are essential components of web applications, ensuring that users can securely access and interact with resources. In Django, implementing user registration, login, logout, password management, and permission control is straightforward, thanks to the built-in authentication and authorization system. By following best practices and leveraging Django's powerful features, you can create secure and reliable web applications that meet the needs of your users and protect their data from unauthorized access.

## Securing User Input and Preventing XSS Attacks in Django

Securing user input and preventing Cross-Site Scripting (XSS) attacks are critical aspects of web application security. In Django full stack development, it's essential to properly sanitize and validate user input to mitigate
```

the risk of XSS vulnerabilities. In this guide, we'll explore best practices and techniques for securing user input and preventing XSS attacks in Django, covering both frontend and backend strategies.

1. Sanitizing User Input in Forms

One of the primary entry points for user input in Django applications is through forms. By properly sanitizing and validating form data, you can reduce the risk of XSS vulnerabilities.

```python
# forms.py

from django import forms
from django.utils.html import escape
from .models import Comment

class CommentForm(forms.ModelForm):
    content = forms.CharField(widget=forms.Textarea)

    def clean_content(self):
        content = self.cleaned_data.get('content')
        return escape(content)

    class Meta:
        model = Comment
```

```
    fields = ['content']
```

In this example, we use Django's form validation mechanism to clean the content field by escaping HTML characters using the `escape` function from `django.utils.html`.

2. Implementing Content Security Policy (CSP)

Content Security Policy (CSP) is a security standard that helps prevent XSS attacks by specifying the trusted sources of content that a browser should execute or render. In Django, you can implement CSP by configuring the appropriate HTTP headers.

```python
# middleware.py

from django.utils.deprecation import MiddlewareMixin

class CSPMiddleware(MiddlewareMixin):
    def process_response(self, request, response):
        response['Content-Security-Policy'] = "default-src 'self'"
        return response
```

By adding a custom middleware to your Django application and configuring the `Content-Security-Policy` header, you can specify trusted sources for scripts, stylesheets, images, fonts, and other types of content.

3. Escaping User Input in Templates

In addition to sanitizing user input in forms, it's essential to properly escape user-generated content when rendering templates to prevent XSS vulnerabilities.

```html
<!-- template.html -->

<div>{{ content|escape }}</div>
```

By using the `escape` template filter, you can ensure that any user-generated content displayed in the template is properly escaped, preventing malicious scripts from executing.

4. Using XSS Protection Headers

Modern web browsers provide built-in XSS protection mechanisms that can help mitigate XSS attacks. In

Django, you can enable XSS protection by configuring the appropriate HTTP headers.

```python
# middleware.py

class XSSProtectionMiddleware(MiddlewareMixin):
    def process_response(self, request, response):
        response['X-XSS-Protection'] = '1; mode=block'
        return response
```

By adding a custom middleware to your Django application and configuring the `X-XSS-Protection` header, you can enable XSS protection in supported browsers, further reducing the risk of XSS vulnerabilities.

5. Validating and Sanitizing URLs and Links

User-provided URLs and links are another common entry point for XSS attacks. In Django, you can validate and sanitize URLs and links using the `url` template filter and the `url` and `reverse` functions in views.

```html
<!-- template.html -->
```

```
<a href="{{ url|urlize }}">{{ link_text }}</a>
```

By using the `urlize` template filter, you can automatically convert plain text URLs into clickable links while ensuring that they are properly validated and sanitized.

Securing user input and preventing XSS attacks are essential aspects of web application security in Django full stack development. By following best practices such as sanitizing user input in forms, implementing Content Security Policy (CSP), escaping user-generated content in templates, using XSS protection headers, and validating and sanitizing URLs and links, you can reduce the risk of XSS vulnerabilities and enhance the security of your Django applications. Remember to stay informed about the latest security threats and updates, and regularly audit your codebase for potential vulnerabilities to ensure the continued security and integrity of your Django applications.

Preventing CSRF Attacks and Session Management in Django

Preventing Cross-Site Request Forgery (CSRF) attacks and managing user sessions are critical aspects of web application security in Django full stack development.

CSRF attacks occur when an attacker tricks a user into executing unauthorized actions on a web application where the user is authenticated. Proper session management ensures that user authentication remains secure and sessions are managed effectively. In this guide, we'll explore best practices and techniques for preventing CSRF attacks and managing user sessions in Django, covering both frontend and backend strategies.

1. Preventing CSRF Attacks

CSRF attacks exploit the trust that a site has in a user's browser by tricking it into making unauthorized requests. In Django, CSRF protection is enabled by default, using a CSRF token to validate that a request originated from the same site where the user is authenticated.

```python
# settings.py

MIDDLEWARE = [

    'django.middleware.csrf.CsrfViewMiddleware',

```

By adding `CsrfViewMiddleware` to your middleware settings, Django automatically includes a CSRF token in forms and AJAX requests, which is then validated on the server side.

```html
<!-- template.html -->

<form method="post">
  {% csrf_token %}
  <!-- Form fields -->
  <button type="submit">Submit</button>
</form>
```

In HTML forms, you can include the `{% csrf_token %}` template tag to include the CSRF token automatically. For AJAX requests, you can add the CSRF token to the request headers.

2. Session Management

Session management in Django involves securely managing user sessions, storing session data, and handling session expiration and invalidation.

```python
# settings.py
```

```
SESSION_ENGINE =
'django.contrib.sessions.backends.db'
SESSION_COOKIE_SECURE = True
SESSION_EXPIRE_AT_BROWSER_CLOSE = True
```

In the `settings.py` file, you can configure the session engine, enable secure session cookies, and set sessions to expire at the end of the user's browser session.

```python
# views.py

from django.contrib.auth import login

def my_login_view(request):
    # Authenticate user
    user = authenticate(request, username=username,
password=password)
    if user is not None:
        # Log user in and create session
        login(request, user)
```

When a user logs in, you can use Django's `login` function to authenticate the user and create a session.

3. Session Expiration and Invalidation

It's important to set session expiration policies to ensure that inactive sessions are automatically expired and to handle session invalidation when a user logs out.

```python
# settings.py

SESSION_COOKIE_AGE = 3600  # 1 hour
```

You can configure the session cookie age in the `settings.py` file to determine how long a session remains active before expiring.

```python
# views.py

from django.contrib.auth import logout

def my_logout_view(request):
    # Log user out and invalidate session
    logout(request)
```

When a user logs out, you can use Django's `logout` function to log the user out and invalidate the session.

4. CSRF Protection for AJAX Requests

When making AJAX requests in Django, you need to include the CSRF token in the request headers to ensure that the request is not blocked by CSRF protection.

```javascript
// script.js

const csrftoken =
document.querySelector('[name=csrfmiddlewaretoken]').
value;

fetch('/api/data/', {
  method: 'POST',
  headers: {
    'Content-Type': 'application/json',
    'X-CSRFToken': csrftoken,
  },
  body: JSON.stringify(data),
});
```

By including the CSRF token in the request headers, you can ensure that AJAX requests are protected against CSRF attacks.

Preventing CSRF attacks and managing user sessions are critical aspects of web application security in Django full stack development. By enabling CSRF protection, configuring secure session management settings, handling session expiration and invalidation, and including the CSRF token in AJAX requests, you can reduce the risk of CSRF vulnerabilities and ensure the security and integrity of your Django applications. Remember to stay informed about the latest security best practices and updates, and regularly audit your codebase for potential vulnerabilities to ensure the continued security of your Django applications.

Best Practices for Secure Coding in Django Full Stack Development

Secure coding is essential for building robust and reliable web applications that protect user data and prevent security vulnerabilities. In Django full stack development, adhering to secure coding best practices is crucial for ensuring the security and integrity of your applications. In this guide, we'll explore key principles and techniques for secure coding in Django, covering both frontend and backend strategies.

1. Principle of Least Privilege

The principle of least privilege states that users and processes should only have access to the resources and permissions necessary to perform their tasks. In Django, apply this principle by restricting user permissions and access controls to the minimum required for their role.

```python
# views.py

from django.contrib.auth.decorators import permission_required

@permission_required('myapp.can_create_article')
def create_article(request):
    # Create article logic
```

By using Django's built-in permission system and decorators, you can enforce the principle of least privilege and restrict access to specific views or functionality based on user permissions.

2. Input Validation and Sanitization

Proper input validation and sanitization are essential for preventing injection attacks such as SQL injection and Cross-Site Scripting (XSS). In Django, validate and sanitize user input using built-in form validation and template filters.

```python
```

```python
# forms.py

from django import forms

class MyForm(forms.Form):
    name = forms.CharField(max_length=100)
```

```html
<!-- template.html -->

<div>{{ user_input|escape }}</div>
```

By using Django's form validation and template filters, you can validate and sanitize user input to prevent injection attacks and protect against security vulnerabilities.

3. Secure Authentication and Authorization

Implement secure authentication and authorization mechanisms to protect user accounts and access controls. Use strong password hashing algorithms, enforce password complexity requirements, and enable multi-factor authentication where possible.

```python
# settings.py
```

```python
PASSWORD_HASHERS = [
    'django.contrib.auth.hashers.Argon2PasswordHasher',

AUTH_PASSWORD_VALIDATORS = [
    {
      'NAME':
'django.contrib.auth.password_validation.MinimumLeng
thValidator',
      'OPTIONS': {'min_length': 8},
```

Additionally, enforce secure session management settings, such as secure session cookies, session expiration, and CSRF protection.

4. Secure Communication

Ensure secure communication between the client and server by using HTTPS (HTTP Secure) for all network communication. Enable SSL/TLS encryption to protect sensitive data transmitted over the network and prevent eavesdropping and man-in-the-middle attacks.

```python
# settings.py

SESSION_COOKIE_SECURE = True
```

```
CSRF_COOKIE_SECURE = True
```

By configuring secure session cookies and enabling HTTPS, you can protect user sessions and prevent session hijacking and interception of sensitive data.

5. Regular Security Audits and Code Reviews

Conduct regular security audits and code reviews to identify and mitigate potential security vulnerabilities in your Django applications. Review code for common security issues such as input validation errors, insecure dependencies, and misconfigurations.

```bash
# Run security audits using security scanning tools
safety check
bandit -r myapp/
```

By using security scanning tools such as Safety and Bandit, you can automate security audits and identify potential vulnerabilities in your Django codebase.

Adhering to secure coding best practices is essential for building secure and reliable Django applications that protect user data and prevent security vulnerabilities. By following principles such as the principle of least privilege, implementing input validation and sanitization, ensuring secure authentication and authorization, enabling secure communication, and conducting regular security audits and code reviews, you can enhance the security and integrity of your Django applications. Remember to stay informed about the latest security threats and updates, and continuously monitor and improve the security posture of your Django codebase to protect against evolving security risks.

Chapter 15

Building Real-World Projects with Django

Project 1: Building a Simple Blog Application with Django

In this project, we'll build a simple blog application using Django, a high-level Python web framework. The blog application will allow users to create, read, update, and delete blog posts, as well as manage user accounts and authentication. By following along with this project, you'll learn how to create models, views, templates, forms, and authentication functionality in Django to build a fully functional web application.

Step 1: Setting Up the Django Project

First, let's set up a new Django project and create a new Django app within the project.

```bash
# Create a new Django project
django-admin startproject myblog_project

# Navigate to the project directory
cd myblog_project

# Create a new Django app
python manage.py startapp blog
```

Step 2: Defining Models

Next, let's define the models for our blog application. We'll create a `Post` model to represent blog posts and a `Profile` model to extend the built-in `User` model for user profiles.

```python
# blog/models.py

from django.db import models
from django.contrib.auth.models import User
```

```python
class Profile(models.Model):
    user = models.OneToOneField(User,
on_delete=models.CASCADE)
    bio = models.TextField(blank=True)

class Post(models.Model):
    title = models.CharField(max_length=200)
    author = models.ForeignKey(User,
on_delete=models.CASCADE)
    content = models.TextField()
    created_at =
models.DateTimeField(auto_now_add=True)
    updated_at = models.DateTimeField(auto_now=True)
```

Step 3: Creating Views

Now, let's create views for our blog application to handle rendering templates and processing user requests.

```python
# blog/views.py

from django.shortcuts import render
from .models import Post

def post_list(request):
```

```python
    posts = Post.objects.all()
    return render(request, 'blog/post_list.html', {'posts':
posts})

def post_detail(request, pk):
    post = Post.objects.get(pk=pk)
    return render(request, 'blog/post_detail.html', {'post':
post})
```

Step 4: Setting Up URLs

We need to define URL patterns for our blog application to map URLs to views.

```python
# blog/urls.py

from django.urls import path
from . import views

urlpatterns = [
    path('', views.post_list, name='post_list'),
    path('post/<int:pk>/', views.post_detail,
name='post_detail'),
]
```

Step 5: Creating Templates

Let's create templates for our blog application to render HTML content.

```html
<!-- blog/templates/blog/post_list.html -->

<!DOCTYPE html>
<html lang="en">
<head>
    <meta charset="UTF-8">
    <title>My Blog - Posts</title>
</head>
<body>
    <h1>Blog Posts</h1>
    {% for post in posts %}
    <div>
        <h2><a href="{% url 'post_detail' post.pk %}">{{ post.title }}</a></h2>
        <p>{{ post.content }}</p>
    </div>
    {% endfor %}
</body>
</html>
```

```html
<!-- blog/templates/blog/post_detail.html -->
```

```html
<!DOCTYPE html>
<html lang="en">
<head>
    <meta charset="UTF-8">
    <title>{{ post.title }}</title>
</head>
<body>
    <h1>{{ post.title }}</h1>
    <p>{{ post.content }}</p>
    <p>Author: {{ post.author }}</p>
</body>
</html>
```

Step 6: Configuring Authentication

Let's configure user authentication for our blog application to allow users to create and manage blog posts.

```python
# settings.py

INSTALLED_APPS = [
    ...
    'django.contrib.auth',
    'django.contrib.sessions',
```

```
    'django.contrib.messages',
    'django.contrib.staticfiles',
    'blog',
]
```

Step 7: Running Migrations and Creating Superuser

Before running the server, let's apply migrations and
create a superuser for accessing the Django admin
interface.

```bash
# Apply migrations
python manage.py migrate

# Create superuser
python manage.py createsuperuser
```

Step 8: Running the Development Server

Finally, let's run the development server and access our
blog application in the web browser.

```bash
# Run the development server
python manage.py runserver
```

```
```

Congratulations! You've successfully built a simple blog application with Django. In this project, you learned how to define models, create views, set up URLs, create templates, configure authentication, and run migrations in Django. You can further enhance this application by adding features such as user registration, comment system, search functionality, and more. Django provides a powerful and flexible framework for building web applications, and with practice and exploration, you can create even more sophisticated and feature-rich web applications using Django.

Project 2: Creating a Dynamic E-commerce Platform with Django

In this project, we'll build a dynamic e-commerce platform using Django, a powerful Python web framework. The e-commerce platform will include features such as product listing, searching, shopping cart functionality, user authentication, and payment integration. By following along with this project, you'll learn how to implement key components of an e-commerce website and gain hands-on experience with Django full stack development.

Step 1: Setting Up the Django Project

First, let's set up a new Django project and create a new Django app within the project.

```bash
# Create a new Django project
django-admin startproject ecommerce_project

# Navigate to the project directory
cd ecommerce_project

# Create a new Django app
python manage.py startapp shop
```

Step 2: Defining Models

Next, let's define the models for our e-commerce platform. We'll create models for products, categories, and orders.

```python
# shop/models.py

from django.db import models
from django.contrib.auth.models import User

class Category(models.Model):
```

```python
    name = models.CharField(max_length=100)

class Product(models.Model):
    name = models.CharField(max_length=200)
    category = models.ForeignKey(Category,
on_delete=models.CASCADE)
    price = models.DecimalField(max_digits=10,
decimal_places=2)
    description = models.TextField()

class Order(models.Model):
    user = models.ForeignKey(User,
on_delete=models.CASCADE)
    products = models.ManyToManyField(Product)
    total_price = models.DecimalField(max_digits=10,
decimal_places=2)
    created_at =
models.DateTimeField(auto_now_add=True)
```

Step 3: Creating Views

Now, let's create views for our e-commerce platform to handle rendering templates and processing user requests.

```python
# shop/views.py
```

```python
from django.shortcuts import render, get_object_or_404
from .models import Product

def product_list(request):
    products = Product.objects.all()
    return render(request, 'shop/product_list.html',
{'products': products})

def product_detail(request, pk):
    product = get_object_or_404(Product, pk=pk)
    return render(request, 'shop/product_detail.html',
{'product': product})
```

Step 4: Setting Up URLs

We need to define URL patterns for our e-commerce platform to map URLs to views.

```python
# shop/urls.py

from django.urls import path
from . import views

urlpatterns = [
    path('', views.product_list, name='product_list'),
```

```
    path('product/<int:pk>/', views.product_detail,
name='product_detail'),
]
```

Step 5: Creating Templates

Let's create templates for our e-commerce platform to
render HTML content.

```html
<!-- shop/templates/shop/product_list.html -->

<!DOCTYPE html>
<html lang="en">
<head>
    <meta charset="UTF-8">
    <title>Product List</title>
</head>
<body>
    <h1>Products</h1>
    {% for product in products %}
    <div>
        <h2><a href="{% url 'product_detail' product.pk
%}">{{ product.name }}</a></h2>
        <p>Price: ${{ product.price }}</p>
    </div>
    {% endfor %}
```

```
</body>
</html>
```

```html
<!-- shop/templates/shop/product_detail.html -->

<!DOCTYPE html>
<html lang="en">
<head>
    <meta charset="UTF-8">
    <title>{{ product.name }}</title>
</head>
<body>
    <h1>{{ product.name }}</h1>
    <p>Description: {{ product.description }}</p>
    <p>Price: ${{ product.price }}</p>
</body>
</html>
```

Step 6: Configuring Authentication

Let's configure user authentication for our e-commerce platform to allow users to create accounts and login.

```python
# settings.py
```

```
INSTALLED_APPS = [
    ...
    'django.contrib.auth',
    'django.contrib.sessions',
    'django.contrib.messages',
    'django.contrib.staticfiles',
    'shop',
]
```

Step 7: Running Migrations and Creating Superuser

Before running the server, let's apply migrations and create a superuser for accessing the Django admin interface.

```bash
# Apply migrations
python manage.py migrate

# Create superuser
python manage.py createsuperuser
```

Step 8: Running the Development Server

Finally, let's run the development server and access our e-commerce platform in the web browser.

```bash
# Run the development server
python manage.py runserver
```

Congratulations! You've successfully built a dynamic e-commerce platform with Django. In this project, you learned how to define models, create views, set up URLs, create templates, configure authentication, and run migrations in Django. You can further enhance this e-commerce platform by adding features such as user registration, shopping cart functionality, checkout process, and payment integration. Django provides a powerful and flexible framework for building web applications, and with practice and exploration, you can create even more sophisticated and feature-rich e-commerce websites using Django.

Project 3: Developing a User-Friendly Portfolio Website with Django

In this optional project, we'll create a user-friendly portfolio website using Django, a versatile Python web framework. A portfolio website serves as a showcase of your work, skills, and experiences, allowing you to

present yourself professionally to potential clients or
employers. By following along with this project, you'll
learn how to design and develop a portfolio website with
Django, incorporating features such as project listing,
skill display, contact form, and more.

Step 1: Setting Up the Django Project

Let's start by setting up a new Django project and
creating a new Django app within the project.

```bash
# Create a new Django project
django-admin startproject portfolio_project

# Navigate to the project directory
cd portfolio_project

# Create a new Django app
python manage.py startapp portfolio
```

Step 2: Defining Models

Next, let's define the models for our portfolio website.
We'll create models for projects, skills, and contact
messages.

```python
# portfolio/models.py

from django.db import models

class Project(models.Model):
    title = models.CharField(max_length=200)
    description = models.TextField()
    image = models.ImageField(upload_to='projects/')
    url = models.URLField()

class Skill(models.Model):
    name = models.CharField(max_length=100)
    description = models.TextField()

class ContactMessage(models.Model):
    name = models.CharField(max_length=100)
    email = models.EmailField()
    message = models.TextField()
    created_at = models.DateTimeField(auto_now_add=True)
```

Step 3: Creating Views

Now, let's create views for our portfolio website to handle rendering templates and processing user requests.

```python
# portfolio/views.py

from django.shortcuts import render, redirect
from .models import Project, Skill, ContactMessage

def project_list(request):
    projects = Project.objects.all()
    return render(request, 'portfolio/project_list.html',
{'projects': projects})

def skill_list(request):
    skills = Skill.objects.all()
    return render(request, 'portfolio/skill_list.html',
{'skills': skills})

def contact_form(request):
    if request.method == 'POST':
        # Process contact form submission
        return redirect('contact_success')
    return render(request, 'portfolio/contact_form.html')

def contact_success(request):
    return render(request, 'portfolio/contact_success.html')
```

Step 4: Setting Up URLs

We need to define URL patterns for our portfolio website to map URLs to views.

```python
# portfolio/urls.py

from django.urls import path
from . import views

urlpatterns = [
    path('projects/', views.project_list,
name='project_list'),
    path('skills/', views.skill_list, name='skill_list'),
    path('contact/', views.contact_form,
name='contact_form'),
    path('contact/success/', views.contact_success,
name='contact_success'),
]
```

Step 5: Creating Templates

Let's create templates for our portfolio website to render HTML content.

```html
<!-- portfolio/templates/portfolio/project_list.html -->
```

```html
<!DOCTYPE html>
<html lang="en">
<head>
   <meta charset="UTF-8">
   <title>Projects</title>
</head>
<body>
   <h1>Projects</h1>
   {% for project in projects %}
   <div>
      <h2><a href="{{ project.url }}">{{ project.title }}</a></h2>
      <p>{{ project.description }}</p>
      <img src="{{ project.image.url }}" alt="{{ project.title }}">
   </div>
   {% endfor %}
</body>
</html>
```

```html
<!-- portfolio/templates/portfolio/skill_list.html -->

<!DOCTYPE html>
<html lang="en">
<head>
   <meta charset="UTF-8">
```

```html
    <title>Skills</title>
</head>
<body>
    <h1>Skills</h1>
    <ul>
    {% for skill in skills %}
        <li>{{ skill.name }}</li>
    {% endfor %}
    </ul>
</body>
</html>
```

```html
<!-- portfolio/templates/portfolio/contact_form.html -->

<!DOCTYPE html>
<html lang="en">
<head>
    <meta charset="UTF-8">
    <title>Contact</title>
</head>
<body>
    <h1>Contact</h1>
    <form method="post">
        {% csrf_token %}
        <input type="text" name="name"
placeholder="Name">
```

```html
        <input type="email" name="email"
placeholder="Email">
        <textarea name="message"
placeholder="Message"></textarea>
        <button type="submit">Send</button>
      </form>
</body>
</html>
```


```html
<!-- portfolio/templates/portfolio/contact_success.html --
>

<!DOCTYPE html>
<html lang="en">
<head>
    <meta charset="UTF-8">
    <title>Contact Success</title>
</head>
<body>
    <h1>Thank you for contacting me!</h1>
</body>
</html>
```

Step 6: Running Migrations and Configuring Static Files

Before running the server, let's apply migrations and configure static files for our portfolio website.

```bash
# Apply migrations
python manage.py migrate
```

```python
# settings.py

STATIC_URL = '/static/'
```

Step 7: Running the Development Server

Finally, let's run the development server and access our portfolio website in the web browser.

```bash
# Run the development server
python manage.py runserver
```

Congratulations! You've successfully built a user-friendly portfolio website with Django. In this project, you learned how to define models, create views, set up URLs, create templates, configure static files, and run migrations in Django. You can further enhance this portfolio website by adding features such as user authentication, project categories, social media integration, and more. Django provides a powerful and flexible framework for building web applications, and with practice and exploration, you can create even more impressive and interactive portfolio websites using Django.

Project 4: Building a Social Networking Application with Django

In this optional project, we'll create a social networking application using Django, a powerful Python web framework. A social networking application allows users to connect, share content, interact with each other, and build communities around shared interests. By following along with this project, you'll learn how to implement key features of a social networking platform, including user registration, profiles, posts, likes, comments, and more.

Step 1: Setting Up the Django Project

Let's start by setting up a new Django project and creating a new Django app within the project.

```bash
```

```
# Create a new Django project
django-admin startproject social_project

# Navigate to the project directory
cd social_project

# Create a new Django app
python manage.py startapp social
```

Step 2: Defining Models

Next, let's define the models for our social networking application. We'll create models for users, posts, likes, and comments.

```python
# social/models.py

from django.db import models
from django.contrib.auth.models import User

class Profile(models.Model):
    user = models.OneToOneField(User,
on_delete=models.CASCADE)
    bio = models.TextField(blank=True)
    avatar = models.ImageField(upload_to='avatars/',
blank=True)
```

```python
class Post(models.Model):
    author = models.ForeignKey(User,
on_delete=models.CASCADE)
    content = models.TextField()
    created_at =
models.DateTimeField(auto_now_add=True)

class Like(models.Model):
    user = models.ForeignKey(User,
on_delete=models.CASCADE)
    post = models.ForeignKey(Post,
on_delete=models.CASCADE)
    created_at =
models.DateTimeField(auto_now_add=True)

class Comment(models.Model):
    user = models.ForeignKey(User,
on_delete=models.CASCADE)
    post = models.ForeignKey(Post,
on_delete=models.CASCADE)
    content = models.TextField()
    created_at =
models.DateTimeField(auto_now_add=True)
```
```

**Step 3: Creating Views**
```

Now, let's create views for our social networking application to handle rendering templates and processing user requests.

```python
# social/views.py

from django.shortcuts import render, redirect
from django.contrib.auth.decorators import login_required
from .models import Post, Like, Comment

@login_required
def home(request):
    posts = Post.objects.all()
    return render(request, 'social/home.html', {'posts': posts})

@login_required
def post_detail(request, pk):
    post = Post.objects.get(pk=pk)
    return render(request, 'social/post_detail.html', {'post': post})

@login_required
def create_post(request):
    if request.method == 'POST':
        # Process post creation form submission
```

```
        return redirect('home')
    return render(request, 'social/create_post.html')
```

Step 4: Setting Up URLs

We need to define URL patterns for our social
networking application to map URLs to views.

```python
# social/urls.py

from django.urls import path
from . import views

urlpatterns = [
    path('', views.home, name='home'),
    path('post/<int:pk>/', views.post_detail,
name='post_detail'),
    path('post/create/', views.create_post,
name='create_post'),
]
```

Step 5: Creating Templates

Let's create templates for our social networking
application to render HTML content.

```html
<!-- social/templates/social/home.html -->

<!DOCTYPE html>
<html lang="en">
<head>
    <meta charset="UTF-8">
    <title>Home</title>
</head>
<body>
    <h1>Home</h1>
    {% for post in posts %}
    <div>
        <h2><a href="{% url 'post_detail' post.pk %}">Post by {{ post.author }}</a></h2>
        <p>{{ post.content }}</p>
    </div>
    {% endfor %}
</body>
</html>
```

```html
<!-- social/templates/social/post_detail.html -->

<!DOCTYPE html>
<html lang="en">
```

```
<head>
  <meta charset="UTF-8">
  <title>{{ post.author }}'s Post</title>
</head>
<body>
  <h1>{{ post.author }}'s Post</h1>
  <p>{{ post.content }}</p>
</body>
</html>
```

```html
<!-- social/templates/social/create_post.html -->

<!DOCTYPE html>
<html lang="en">
<head>
  <meta charset="UTF-8">
  <title>Create Post</title>
</head>
<body>
  <h1>Create Post</h1>
  <form method="post">
    {% csrf_token %}
    <textarea name="content" placeholder="Enter your post"></textarea>
    <button type="submit">Post</button>
  </form>
```

```
</body>
</html>
```

Step 6: Configuring Authentication

Let's configure user authentication for our social
networking application to allow users to create accounts
and login.

```python
# settings.py

INSTALLED_APPS = [
    ...
    'django.contrib.auth',
    'django.contrib.sessions',
    'django.contrib.messages',
    'django.contrib.staticfiles',
    'social',
]
```

Step 7: Running Migrations and Configuring Static Files

Before running the server, let's apply migrations and configure static files for our social networking application.

```bash
# Apply migrations
python manage.py migrate
```

```python
# settings.py

STATIC_URL = '/static/'
```

Step 8: Running the Development Server

Finally, let's run the development server and access our social networking application in the web browser.

```bash
# Run the development server
python manage.py runserver
```

Congratulations! You've successfully built a social networking application with Django. In this project, you learned how to define models, create views, set up URLs, create templates, configure static files, and run migrations in Django. You can further enhance this social networking application by adding features such as user profiles, likes, comments, friend requests, messaging, and more. Django provides a powerful and flexible framework for building web applications, and with practice and exploration, you can create even more engaging and interactive social networking platforms using Django.

Chapter 16

Beyond the Basics: Exploring Advanced Django Features (Optional)

Introduction to Django REST Framework (Building APIs)

Django REST Framework (DRF) is a powerful toolkit for building Web APIs with Django, a high-level Python web framework. With DRF, you can easily create APIs that follow the RESTful architectural style, allowing you to interact with your Django applications programmatically. In this guide, we'll introduce you to Django REST Framework and walk you through the process of building APIs with code examples and best practices.

What is Django REST Framework?

Django REST Framework is a flexible toolkit for building Web APIs in Django. It provides a set of powerful features and tools that simplify the creation of APIs, including serialization, authentication, permissions, viewsets, and routers. DRF is built on top of Django's class-based views, making it easy to integrate with existing Django applications.

Installation

First, let's install Django REST Framework using pip, the Python package manager.

```bash

pip install djangorestframework
```

Once installed, add "rest_framework" to the `INSTALLED_APPS` list in your Django project's `settings.py` file.

```python

# settings.py

INSTALLED_APPS = [

    'rest_framework',

```

Serializers

Serializers in Django REST Framework convert complex data types, such as querysets and model instances, into native Python data types that can be easily rendered into JSON, XML, or other content types. Let's create a serializer for a simple model.

```python

# serializers.py

from rest_framework import serializers

from .models import MyModel
```

```python
class MyModelSerializer(serializers.ModelSerializer):

    class Meta:

        model = MyModel

        fields = ['id', 'name', 'description']
```

Views

Views in Django REST Framework are similar to Django's views, but they are specifically designed to work with APIs. Let's create a simple view to retrieve a list of objects.

```python
# views.py

from rest_framework import generics

from .models import MyModel

from .serializers import MyModelSerializer

class MyModelListView(generics.ListAPIView):

    queryset = MyModel.objects.all()

    serializer_class = MyModelSerializer
```

URLs

To expose our API endpoints, we need to define URL patterns for our views.

```python
# urls.py

from django.urls import path

from . import views

urlpatterns = [

    path('api/mymodels/',
views.MyModelListView.as_view(), name='mymodel-list'),

```

Authentication and Permissions

Django REST Framework provides built-in support for authentication and permissions, allowing you to control access to your API endpoints. Let's add authentication and permissions to our views.

```python
# views.py

from rest_framework import generics, permissions

from .models import MyModel
```

```python
from .serializers import MyModelSerializer

class MyModelListView(generics.ListAPIView):

    queryset = MyModel.objects.all()

    serializer_class = MyModelSerializer

    permission_classes = [permissions.IsAuthenticated]
```

Pagination

DRF also supports pagination out of the box, allowing you to control how many objects are returned in each API response.

```python
# settings.py

REST_FRAMEWORK = {

    'DEFAULT_PAGINATION_CLASS': 'rest_framework.pagination.PageNumberPagination',

    'PAGE_SIZE': 10
```

Testing

Django REST Framework provides a powerful set of testing utilities for testing your API endpoints. Let's write a simple test for our view.

```python
```

```python
# tests.py

from django.urls import reverse

from rest_framework.test import APITestCase

class MyModelListViewTestCase(APITestCase):

    def test_list_view(self):

        url = reverse('mymodel-list')

        response = self.client.get(url)

        self.assertEqual(response.status_code, 200)
```

Django REST Framework is a powerful toolkit for building Web APIs in Django. In this guide, we introduced you to DRF and walked you through the process of building APIs with code examples and best practices. With DRF, you can easily create APIs that follow the RESTful architectural style, allowing you to interact with your Django applications programmatically. Whether you're building a simple API for a mobile application or a complex API for a web application, Django REST Framework provides the tools and features you need to get the job done efficiently and effectively.

Working with Django Forms for Complex User Input

Django provides a powerful forms library that allows developers to easily handle user input, validate data, and interact with databases. In this guide, we'll explore how to work with Django forms for complex user input scenarios, covering various form features, validation techniques, formsets, and form customization.

Introduction to Django Forms

Django forms are Python classes that represent HTML forms. They handle form rendering, data validation, and data cleaning. Django forms are typically defined in a `forms.py` module within a Django app.

Defining a Simple Form

Let's start by defining a simple form for collecting user input. We'll create a form for a contact page with fields for name, email, and message.

```python
# forms.py

from django import forms

class ContactForm(forms.Form):

    name = forms.CharField(max_length=100)
```

email = forms.EmailField()

message = forms.CharField(widget=forms.Textarea)

Rendering a Form in a Template

To render the form in a template, we need to instantiate the form object and pass it to the template context.

```html
<!-- contact_form.html -->
<!DOCTYPE html>
<html lang="en">
<head>
    <meta charset="UTF-8">
    <title>Contact Form</title>
</head>
<body>
    <h1>Contact Us</h1>
    <form method="post">
        {% csrf_token %}
        {{ form.as_p }}
```

```html
    <button type="submit">Submit</button>

  </form>

</body>

</html>
```

Processing Form Submission

In the view function, we need to handle form submission and perform data validation.

```python
# views.py

from django.shortcuts import render

from .forms import ContactForm

def contact_form(request):

    if request.method == 'POST':

        form = ContactForm(request.POST)

        if form.is_valid():

            # Process form data

            name = form.cleaned_data['name']
```

email = form.cleaned_data['email']

message = form.cleaned_data['message']

Additional logic (e.g., sending email)

return render(request, 'success.html')

else:

form = ContactForm()

return render(request, 'contact_form.html', {'form': form})

Customizing Form Field Rendering

Django forms provide flexibility for customizing form field rendering using widgets and templates.

```python
# forms.py

class CustomizedContactForm(ContactForm):

    def __init__(self, args, kwargs):

        super().__init__(args, kwargs)

        self.fields['name'].widget.attrs['class'] = 'form-control'
```

```python
        self.fields['email'].widget.attrs['class'] = 'form-
control'

        self.fields['message'].widget.attrs['class'] = 'form-
control'

        self.fields['message'].widget.attrs['rows'] = 5
```

Form Validation and Error Handling

Django forms perform data validation automatically
based on field types and constraints. You can also define
custom validation logic using form methods.

```python
# forms.py

class LoginForm(forms.Form):

    username = forms.CharField(max_length=100)

    password =
forms.CharField(widget=forms.PasswordInput)

    def clean(self):

        cleaned_data = super().clean()

        username = cleaned_data.get('username')

        password = cleaned_data.get('password')

        # Custom validation logic
```

```python
    if not username:

        raise forms.ValidationError("Username is
required.")

    if not password:

        raise forms.ValidationError("Password is
required.")
```

Working with Formsets

Django formsets allow you to work with multiple forms
on the same page. This is useful for scenarios such as
creating multiple instances of a model.

```python
# forms.py

from django.forms import formset_factory

from .models import MyModel

MyModelFormSet = formset_factory(MyModelForm,
extra=2)
```

Django forms provide a powerful toolset for handling
complex user input scenarios in web applications. In this
guide, we've covered the basics of working with Django

forms, including form definition, rendering, processing form submissions, customizing form rendering, form validation, error handling, and working with formsets. With Django forms, you can create user-friendly and robust web forms that meet the requirements of your application. Whether you're building a simple contact form or a complex data entry form, Django forms provide the flexibility and functionality you need to streamline the user input process.

Building Custom Django Admin Interfaces

Django's built-in admin interface is powerful and flexible, allowing developers to manage models, data, and user permissions with ease. However, there are cases where you may need to customize the admin interface to better suit your application's requirements or provide a more user-friendly experience. In this guide, we'll explore how to build custom Django admin interfaces, covering various customization techniques, such as overriding templates, customizing admin views, and adding custom functionality.

Introduction to Django Admin Interface

The Django admin interface is an automatic admin interface that Django creates for models registered with `admin.site.register()`. It provides CRUD (Create, Read, Update, Delete) operations for managing model instances and integrates with Django's authentication and permission system.

Basic Customization

Model Admin Options

You can customize the behavior of the admin interface by defining a custom `ModelAdmin` class for your models. This allows you to specify display options, list filters, search fields, and more.

```python
# admin.py

from django.contrib import admin

from .models import MyModel

class MyModelAdmin(admin.ModelAdmin):
    list_display = ['field1', 'field2', ...]

    list_filter = ['field1', 'field2', ...]

    search_fields = ['field1', 'field2', ...]

admin.site.register(MyModel, MyModelAdmin)
```

Customizing Templates

You can override the default admin templates to customize the appearance and layout of the admin interface. Create a directory named `admin` in your templates directory and place your custom admin templates inside it.

```html
<!-- templates/admin/base_site.html -->

{% extends "admin/base_site.html" %}

{% block title %}

   My Custom Admin Interface

{% endblock %}
```

Advanced Customization

Custom Admin Views

You can create custom admin views by subclassing
`AdminSite` and defining custom view methods. This
allows you to add custom functionality to the admin
interface, such as custom reports or dashboard views.

```python
# admin.py

from django.contrib.admin import AdminSite

from django.http import HttpResponse

class CustomAdminSite(AdminSite):

   def custom_view(self, request):
```

```python
    # Custom view logic

    return HttpResponse("Hello, Custom Admin
View!")

custom_admin_site =
CustomAdminSite(name='customadmin')

# Register models with custom admin site

custom_admin_site.register(MyModel,
MyModelAdmin)
```

Inline Model Admin

You can use inline model admins to edit related model
instances directly from the parent model's admin
interface. This is useful for managing related data in a
single view.

```python
# admin.py

from django.contrib import admin

from .models import ParentModel, ChildModel

class ChildModelInline(admin.TabularInline):

    model = ChildModel
```

```python
class ParentModelAdmin(admin.ModelAdmin):

    inlines = [ChildModelInline]

admin.site.register(ParentModel, ParentModelAdmin)
```

Custom Admin Actions

You can define custom admin actions to perform bulk operations on selected model instances in the admin interface. This allows you to add custom functionality, such as batch processing or data export.

```python
# admin.py

from django.contrib import admin

from .models import MyModel

class MyModelAdmin(admin.ModelAdmin):

    actions = ['custom_action']

    def custom_action(self, request, queryset):

        # Custom action logic

        pass

admin.site.register(MyModel, MyModelAdmin)
```

```

```

Customizing the Django admin interface allows you to tailor the admin experience to meet the specific needs of your application and users. In this guide, we've covered various customization techniques, including model admin options, template overriding, custom admin views, inline model admins, and custom admin actions. With these techniques, you can create custom admin interfaces that provide a more intuitive and efficient user experience for managing data in your Django applications. Whether you're building a simple content management system or a complex enterprise application, Django's flexible admin interface customization capabilities make it easy to create admin interfaces that fit your requirements.

Integrating Third-Party Libraries and Services in Django

Integrating third-party libraries and services into your Django project can greatly enhance its functionality and save development time. In this guide, we'll explore how to integrate third-party libraries and services into a Django project, covering installation, configuration, and usage with code examples and best practices.

Third-party libraries and services offer a wide range of features and functionalities that can complement Django's capabilities. Whether you need to add authentication, payment processing, image manipulation, or any other functionality, chances are there's a third-party library or service that can help.

Installation

To integrate a third-party library or service into your Django project, you'll first need to install it using a package manager like pip. Make sure to check the documentation for the specific library or service for installation instructions.

```bash
pip install <library_name>
```

Configuration

Once installed, you may need to configure the third-party library or service to work with your Django project. This usually involves adding configuration settings to your project's settings file (`settings.py`).

```python
# settings.py

# Example configuration for a third-party library

THIRD_PARTY_API_KEY = 'your_api_key'
```

Usage

After installation and configuration, you can start using the third-party library or service in your Django project.

This typically involves importing the library's modules or classes and using them in your code.

```python
# Example usage of a third-party library

from third_party_library import SomeClass

instance = SomeClass()

result = instance.some_method()
```

Common Integration Scenarios

Authentication

Integrating third-party authentication providers, such as OAuth or social media logins, can streamline the user authentication process in your Django project.

```python
# settings.py

# Example configuration for Django OAuth Toolkit

OAUTH2_PROVIDER = {

    'SCOPES': {'read': 'Read scope', 'write': 'Write scope', 'groups': 'Access to your groups'},

    'CLIENT_ID_GENERATOR_CLASS': 'oauth2_provider.generators.ClientIdGenerator',
```

```
'CLIENT_SECRET_GENERATOR_CLASS':
'oauth2_provider.generators.ClientSecretGenerator',
```

Payment Processing

Integrating payment processing services, such as Stripe or PayPal, can enable secure and convenient payment options for your Django project.

```python

# settings.py

# Example configuration for Stripe

STRIPE_PUBLIC_KEY = 'your_public_key'

STRIPE_SECRET_KEY = 'your_secret_key'
```

Image Manipulation

Integrating image manipulation libraries, such as Pillow or django-imagekit, can add image processing capabilities to your Django project.

```python

# settings.py

# Example configuration for django-imagekit
```

IMAGEKIT_DEFAULT_CACHEFILE_STRATEGY =
'imagekit.cachefiles.strategies.Optimistic'

Best Practices

- **Read the Documentation:** Always refer to the documentation of the third-party library or service for installation, configuration, and usage instructions.
- **Use Virtual Environments:** Utilize virtual environments (e.g., virtualenv or venv) to manage dependencies and isolate project environments.
- **Version Compatibility:** Ensure that the version of the third-party library or service you're integrating is compatible with your Django project's version.
- **Security**: Keep sensitive information, such as API keys or secret tokens, secure by storing them in environment variables or a secure location.

Integrating third-party libraries and services into your Django project can extend its functionality and provide solutions to common development challenges. In this guide, we've covered the process of integrating third-party libraries and services, including installation, configuration, and usage, with code examples and best practices. By leveraging third-party libraries and services, you can enhance your Django project's capabilities and deliver more robust and feature-rich applications to your users.

Chapter 17

Django documentation and community forums

Django's documentation and community forums play a vital role in supporting developers and fostering collaboration within the Django ecosystem. In this guide, we'll explore the Django documentation, including its structure, content, and how to effectively use it. We'll also delve into community forums, such as the Django Users Google Group and Stack Overflow, and discuss their significance in helping developers solve problems and share knowledge.

Django Documentation

Structure

The Django documentation is organized into several sections, each covering different aspects of Django development:

1. Introduction: Provides an overview of Django and its features.

2. Installation: Guides users through the process of installing Django and setting up a development environment.

3. Tutorial: Walks users through creating a simple Django project, covering topics such as models, views, templates, and forms.

4. Topic Guides: Dive deeper into specific topics, such as database models, forms, authentication, and more.

5. API Reference: Detailed documentation for all Django modules, classes, functions, and settings.

6. How-to Guides: Provides step-by-step instructions for common tasks and scenarios, such as deploying Django applications, internationalization, and security.

7. Contributing: Guidelines for contributing to Django's development and documentation.

Content

The Django documentation covers a wide range of topics, from basic concepts to advanced techniques. Some key areas include:

1. Models and database queries
2. Views and URL routing
3. Templates and template tags
4. Forms and form processing
5. Authentication and authorization
6. Middleware and request/response handling
7. Deployment and server configurations
8. Testing and debugging

Using the Django Documentation Effectively

Search Functionality

The Django documentation includes a powerful search functionality that allows users to quickly find relevant information. The search bar at the top of each page enables users to search the entire documentation or restrict the search to specific sections.

Version Switcher

Django maintains documentation for multiple versions, allowing users to access documentation relevant to their Django version. The version switcher dropdown at the bottom of each page enables users to switch between different versions of the documentation.

Examples and Code Snippets

The Django documentation provides numerous examples and code snippets to illustrate concepts and demonstrate best practices. These examples are often accompanied by explanations and annotations to help users understand how to apply them in their projects.

Community Interaction

The Django documentation is open-source and hosted on GitHub, allowing users to contribute improvements, corrections, and additions. Users can submit pull requests to suggest changes to the documentation, report issues, or participate in discussions on GitHub.

Community Forums

Django Users Google Group

The Django Users Google Group is a mailing list where users can ask questions, seek help, and share knowledge with other Django developers. It serves as a valuable resource for developers of all skill levels to interact with the Django community and get assistance with their projects.

Stack Overflow

Stack Overflow is a popular Q&A platform where developers can ask questions and find answers on a wide range of topics, including Django development. The Django tag on Stack Overflow is actively monitored by the Django community, and developers can expect prompt responses to their questions.

Best Practices for Using Community Forums

Search Before Posting

Before posting a question on a community forum, it's advisable to search the forum's archives and existing questions to see if your question has already been answered. Often, someone else may have encountered a similar issue and found a solution.

Provide Context

When asking a question on a community forum, provide as much context and detail as possible. Include relevant code snippets, error messages, and steps you've taken to troubleshoot the issue. This helps others understand the problem and provide accurate assistance.

Follow Forum Guidelines

Each community forum may have its own set of guidelines and etiquette. Be sure to familiarize yourself with the forum's rules before participating, and adhere to them when posting questions or replies.

Contribute and Give Back

Community forums thrive on collaboration and mutual support. Consider contributing to the community by answering questions, sharing knowledge, and helping others solve problems. By giving back to the community, you contribute to its growth and sustainability.

The Django documentation and community forums are invaluable resources for developers working with Django. The documentation provides comprehensive guidance and reference material for all aspects of Django development, while community forums offer opportunities for interaction, collaboration, and support. By leveraging these resources effectively, developers can enhance their Django skills, troubleshoot issues, and become active participants in the Django community.

Exploring Advanced Web Development Topics with Django

Advanced web development with Django encompasses a broad range of topics, from optimizing performance and scalability to implementing complex features and integrating with cutting-edge technologies. In this guide, we'll delve into several advanced topics in Django development, including asynchronous programming, caching, background tasks, web sockets, GraphQL, and more. We'll provide code examples and practical insights to help you leverage these advanced techniques in your Django projects effectively.

1. Asynchronous Programming with Django

Background

Asynchronous programming allows your Django application to handle multiple tasks concurrently, improving performance and responsiveness. Django 3.1 introduced asynchronous views and middleware support using Python's `async` and `await` keywords.

Example

```python
# views.py

from django.http import JsonResponse

import asyncio

async def async_view(request):

    async def inner():

        await asyncio.sleep(1)
```

```python
    return {'message': 'Async response'}

response = await inner()

return JsonResponse(response)
```

urls.py

```python
from django.urls import path

from .views import async_view

urlpatterns = [

    path('async/', async_view),
```

```
```

2. Caching

Background

Caching helps reduce database queries and speeds up response times by storing frequently accessed data in memory or a dedicated cache server. Django provides built-in support for caching using various backends, including memory, file-based, database, and third-party caches like Redis or Memcached.

Example

```python
# settings.py
```

CACHES = {

  'default': {

    'BACKEND':
'django.core.cache.backends.memcached.MemcachedCache',

    'LOCATION': '127.0.0.1:11211',

3. Background Tasks with Celery

Background

Celery is a distributed task queue that allows you to run background tasks asynchronously in Django. It's commonly used for tasks such as sending emails, processing data, or performing periodic tasks.

Example

```python
# tasks.py

from celery import shared_task

@shared_task

def send_email_task():

    # Task logic to send email

    pass
```

```python
# views.py

from .tasks import send_email_task

def send_email(request):

    send_email_task.delay()

    return HttpResponse("Email sent asynchronously")
```

4. WebSockets with Django Channels

Background

Django Channels enables you to handle WebSockets and other real-time communication protocols in Django applications. It provides support for asynchronous consumer classes and integrates seamlessly with Django's authentication and session frameworks.

Example

```python
# consumers.py

from channels.generic.websocket import AsyncWebsocketConsumer

class ChatConsumer(AsyncWebsocketConsumer):

    async def connect(self):
```

```python
        # WebSocket connection logic

        pass

    async def receive(self, text_data=None,
bytes_data=None):

        # WebSocket message handling logic

        pass

    async def disconnect(self, close_code):

        # WebSocket disconnection logic

        pass

# routing.py

from django.urls import re_path

from . import consumers

websocket_urlpatterns = [

    re_path(r'ws/chat/$',
consumers.ChatConsumer.as_asgi()),

```

5. GraphQL Integration with Graphene-Django

Background

GraphQL is a query language for APIs that enables clients to request exactly the data they need. Graphene-Django is a Django integration for GraphQL, allowing you to define GraphQL schemas and resolve queries using Django models and views.

Example

```python
# schema.py

import graphene

from graphene_django.types import DjangoObjectType

from .models import MyModel

class MyModelType(DjangoObjectType):
    class Meta:
        model = MyModel

class Query(graphene.ObjectType):
    my_models = graphene.List(MyModelType)

    def resolve_my_models(self, info):
        return MyModel.objects.all()

schema = graphene.Schema(query=Query)
```

```
```

Advanced web development with Django opens up a world of possibilities for building high-performance, scalable, and real-time web applications. In this guide, we've explored several advanced topics in Django development, including asynchronous programming, caching, background tasks, WebSockets, and GraphQL integration. By mastering these techniques and leveraging the power of Django's ecosystem, you can create sophisticated web applications that meet the demands of modern web development.

Building a Successful Career as a Web Developer with Django

Embarking on a career as a web developer requires dedication, continuous learning, and the acquisition of both technical and soft skills. With the popularity of Django for full-stack web development, aspiring developers can leverage its robust features to build scalable and feature-rich web applications. In this guide, we'll outline the steps to building a successful career as a web developer with Django, including learning paths, practical projects, career advancement tips, and essential skills.

Learning Path

1. Fundamentals of Web Development

Start by learning the fundamentals of web development, including HTML, CSS, and JavaScript. Understanding these core technologies forms the foundation for building web applications.

2. Python Programming

Master Python programming language, as Django is built using Python. Learn Python syntax, data structures, object-oriented programming, and common libraries.

3. Django Framework

Dive into the Django framework by studying its documentation, tutorials, and official resources. Learn about models, views, templates, forms, authentication, and other key concepts.

4. Full-Stack Development

Explore full-stack development with Django by integrating frontend frameworks like React, Vue.js, or Angular for dynamic user interfaces.

5. Advanced Topics

Delve into advanced topics such as asynchronous programming, RESTful APIs, GraphQL, testing, optimization, security, and deployment.

Practical Projects

1. Portfolio Website

Build a personal portfolio website to showcase your skills, projects, and achievements. Use Django to create dynamic pages and showcase your proficiency in web development.

2. Blogging Platform

Create a blogging platform using Django where users can write, publish, and manage blog posts. Implement features like user authentication, comments, and RSS feeds.

3. E-commerce Store

Develop an e-commerce store with Django to learn about product listings, shopping carts, payments, order processing, and user accounts.

4. Social Networking Platform

Build a social networking platform similar to Facebook or Twitter using Django. Implement features like user profiles, friend connections, news feeds, and messaging.

5. Real-World Client Projects

Work on real-world client projects or contribute to open-source projects to gain practical experience and expand your portfolio.

Career Advancement Tips

1. Continuous Learning

Stay updated with the latest technologies, trends, and best practices in web development. Invest time in learning new frameworks, libraries, and tools.

2. Specialization

Consider specializing in a niche area of web development, such as frontend development, backend development, DevOps, or UX/UI design.

3. Networking

Attend web development meetups, conferences, and workshops to network with industry professionals and expand your connections.

4. Freelancing

Explore freelancing opportunities to gain diverse experience, build a client base, and hone your project management and communication skills.

5. Certification

Obtain certifications in web development, Django, or related technologies to validate your skills and enhance your credibility in the job market.

Essential Skills

1. Problem-Solving

Develop strong problem-solving skills to tackle complex challenges and troubleshoot issues in web development projects.

2. Collaboration

Learn to collaborate effectively with designers, developers, clients, and stakeholders to deliver successful web projects.

3. Time Management

Master time management techniques to prioritize tasks, meet deadlines, and efficiently manage project timelines.

4. Communication

Improve communication skills to articulate ideas, convey technical concepts, and collaborate effectively with team members and clients.

5. Adaptability

Stay adaptable and flexible to embrace new technologies, methodologies, and changes in the web development landscape.

Building a successful career as a web developer with Django requires a combination of technical expertise, practical experience, continuous learning, and soft skills development. By following a structured learning path, working on practical projects, leveraging career advancement tips, and honing essential skills, you can carve out a rewarding career in web development. With Django's versatility and your dedication, you'll be well-equipped to tackle challenges, innovate, and thrive in the dynamic field of web development.

Conclusion

Django full stack development offers a comprehensive framework for building robust web applications, encompassing both frontend and backend development. With Django, developers can leverage its powerful features to streamline the development process and create scalable, secure, and feature-rich web applications. Let's explore some key aspects of Django full stack development:

Backend Development with Django

Django provides a solid foundation for backend development, offering features such as:

1. Models and ORM

Django's ORM (Object-Relational Mapping) simplifies database management by allowing developers to define models as Python classes. These models represent database tables and facilitate database operations without writing SQL queries directly.

2. Views and URL Routing

Views in Django handle requests from clients and generate responses. URL routing maps URLs to view functions, enabling developers to create clean and structured URLs for different parts of the application.

3. Templates

Django's template engine allows developers to build dynamic HTML templates with template tags and filters. Templates can be rendered with context data to generate dynamic content for web pages.

Frontend Development with Django

While Django excels in backend development, it also integrates seamlessly with frontend frameworks and technologies:

1. Django Templates

Django's built-in template engine enables developers to create HTML templates with dynamic content using Django template language. Templates can include variables, loops, conditionals, and template inheritance.

2. Integrating JavaScript Frameworks

Django can work with popular frontend JavaScript frameworks like React, Vue.js, or Angular. Developers can build interactive user interfaces with these frameworks while Django handles backend logic and data management.

Database Management

Django supports various database backends, including PostgreSQL, MySQL, SQLite, and Oracle. Developers can choose the most suitable database for their application's requirements and easily manage database operations with Django's ORM.

Security Features

Django prioritizes security and provides built-in features to protect web applications against common security vulnerabilities:

- **Cross-Site Scripting (XSS) Protection:** Django's template system automatically escapes output to prevent XSS attacks.
- **Cross-Site Request Forgery (CSRF) Protection:** Django includes CSRF protection middleware to prevent CSRF attacks by adding a unique token to each form submission.
- **Authentication and Authorization:** Django offers robust authentication and authorization mechanisms, including user authentication, session management, and permission control.

Deployment and Scalability

Django applications can be deployed to various hosting platforms, including traditional servers, cloud platforms like AWS, Heroku, or Azure, and containerization platforms like Docker. Additionally, Django's scalability features, such as caching, database optimization, and load balancing, ensure applications can handle increased traffic and user load effectively.

Django full stack development empowers developers to build modern web applications with ease, combining the power of backend and frontend development within a single framework. With Django's rich feature set, robust security measures, and scalability options, developers can create sophisticated web applications that meet the demands of today's digital landscape. Whether you're building a simple blog, an e-commerce platform, or a complex enterprise application, Django provides the tools and flexibility needed to bring your ideas to life.

Appendix

A Crash Course in Python for Beginners in Django Full Stack Development

Python is a versatile and beginner-friendly programming language widely used in web development, data science, machine learning, and more. In this crash course, we'll cover the basics of Python programming for those new to programming, with a focus on Django full stack development. We'll cover fundamental concepts, syntax, data types, control structures, functions, and more, with code examples tailored to Django development.

Introduction to Python

Python is a high-level, interpreted programming language known for its simplicity and readability. It's an excellent choice for beginners due to its easy-to-understand syntax and extensive libraries.

Installing Python

You can download and install Python from the official website: [python.org](https://www.python.org/). Follow the installation instructions for your operating system.

Running Python Code

Python code can be executed in two ways: using the Python interpreter interactively or by running Python scripts.

```python
# Interactive mode
$ python
>>> print("Hello, world!")
# Running a script
$ python script.py
```

Python Basics

1. Variables and Data Types

Python variables store data of different types. Common data types include integers, floats, strings, lists, tuples, dictionaries, and booleans.

```python
# Variables and data types
name = "John"
age = 30
height = 5.11
is_student = True
```

```
```

2. Control Structures

Control structures like if statements, loops, and conditional expressions control the flow of execution in Python code.

```python
# If statement

if age >= 18:

    print("You are an adult")

else:

    print("You are a minor")

# For loop

for i in range(5):

    print(i)

# While loop

count = 0

while count < 5:

    print(count)
```

```
    count += 1
```

3. Functions

Functions in Python are blocks of reusable code that perform a specific task. They can take parameters and return values.

```python
# Function definition

def greet(name):

    return f"Hello, {name}!"

# Function call

message = greet("Alice")

print(message)
```

Django Full Stack Development with Python

Now, let's apply these Python basics to Django full stack development:

1. Creating a Django Project

Use the Django command-line tool to create a new Django project:

```bash
$ django-admin startproject myproject
```

2. Defining Models

Define database models using Django's ORM in the `models.py` file of your Django app:

```python
# models.py

from django.db import models

class Product(models.Model):
    name = models.CharField(max_length=100)
    price = models.DecimalField(max_digits=10, decimal_places=2)
    description = models.TextField()

    def __str__(self):
        return self.name
```

3. Creating Views

Create views to handle HTTP requests and generate responses in Django:

```python
# views.py

from django.shortcuts import render

from .models import Product

def product_list(request):

    products = Product.objects.all()

    return render(request, 'product_list.html', {'products': products})
```

4. Designing Templates

Design HTML templates to display data dynamically using Django's template language:

```html
<!-- product_list.html -->

<!DOCTYPE html>

<html lang="en">

<head>

    <meta charset="UTF-8">
```

```html
<title>Product List</title>
</head>
<body>
    <h1>Products</h1>
    <ul>
        {% for product in products %}
        <li>{{ product.name }} - ${{ product.price }}</li>
        {% endfor %}
    </ul>
</body>
</html>
```

5. Configuring URLs

Configure URL patterns to map URLs to views in Django's `urls.py` file:

```python
# urls.py

from django.urls import path

from .views import product_list
```

urlpatterns = [

    path('products/', product_list, name='product_list'),

6. Running the Django Development Server

Start the Django development server to test your Django application locally:

```bash
$ python manage.py runserver
```

Python is a versatile and beginner-friendly programming language that serves as the foundation for Django full stack development. In this crash course, we covered the basics of Python programming, including variables, data types, control structures, functions, and more. We then applied these concepts to Django development by creating a Django project, defining models, creating views, designing templates, configuring URLs, and running the development server. With this foundation, you can start your journey into Django full stack development and build powerful web applications with ease.

A Glossary of Key Web Development Terms for Django Full Stack Development

Web development encompasses a vast array of concepts, technologies, and methodologies. Understanding the terminology used in web development, especially within the context of Django full stack development, is crucial for developers to communicate effectively and navigate the development process efficiently. Below is a comprehensive glossary of key terms used in web development, tailored specifically for Django developers.

1. Django:

1. **Definition**: Django is a high-level Python web framework that facilitates rapid development of secure and scalable web applications.
2. **Usage**: Django provides a robust set of tools and conventions for building web applications, including models, views, templates, forms, authentication, and more.

2. Model-View-Template (MVT):

1. **Definition**: MVT is Django's architectural pattern, similar to Model-View-Controller (MVC), where models represent data, views handle business logic, and templates render HTML.
2. **Usage**: Understanding the MVT pattern helps developers organize their codebase and separate

concerns between data, logic, and presentation layers.

3. ORM (Object-Relational Mapping):

1. **Definition**: ORM is a technique for mapping database objects to Python objects, allowing developers to interact with databases using Python objects and methods.
2. **Usage**: Django's built-in ORM abstracts away the complexities of database interactions, enabling developers to work with databases using Python syntax and conventions.

4. Middleware:

1. **Definition**: Middleware are reusable components in Django that enable processing of HTTP requests and responses.
2. **Usage**: Middleware can perform tasks such as authentication, logging, error handling, and request/response manipulation, enhancing the functionality and behavior of Django applications.

5. Admin Interface:

1. **Definition**: Django provides a built-in admin interface for managing models, data, and user permissions.
2. Usage: The admin interface allows administrators and developers to perform CRUD (Create, Read,

Update, Delete) operations on database records, making it easy to manage application data.

6. URL Routing:

1. **Definition**: URL routing is the process of mapping URLs to views in Django, determining which view function should handle a particular URL pattern.
2. **Usage**: URL routing defines the structure of a Django application's URLs and enables navigation between different views and pages.

7. Template Language:

1. **Definition**: Django's template language is a lightweight markup language used to generate dynamic HTML content in Django templates.
2. **Usage**: Template language tags and filters allow developers to include logic, variables, loops, conditionals, and template inheritance in HTML templates, enabling dynamic content generation.

8. Static Files:

1. **Definition**: Static files are files such as CSS, JavaScript, images, and other assets that are served directly to clients without processing by the server.
2. **Usage**: Django provides tools for managing static files, including collecting, serving, and caching static assets to enhance performance and improve user experience.

9. Forms:

1. **Definition**: Forms in Django are Python classes used to define the structure and behavior of HTML forms.
2. **Usage**: Django forms simplify form handling by providing validation, input processing, error handling, and rendering capabilities, reducing the complexity of form-related tasks in web applications.

10. Authentication and Authorization:

1. **Definition**: Authentication is the process of verifying the identity of users, while authorization determines what actions users are allowed to perform within an application.
2. **Usage**: Django provides built-in authentication and authorization mechanisms, including user authentication, session management, permissions, and user groups, ensuring secure access control in web applications.

11. RESTful APIs (Application Programming Interfaces):

1. **Definition**: RESTful APIs are APIs that adhere to the principles of Representational State Transfer (REST), allowing clients to interact with server resources using standard HTTP methods.
2. **Usage**: Django supports building RESTful APIs using third-party packages like Django REST Framework, enabling developers to create APIs

for data exchange and integration with external systems.

12. Asynchronous Programming:

1. **Definition**: Asynchronous programming allows multiple tasks to be executed concurrently, improving performance and responsiveness in web applications.
2. **Usage**: Django supports asynchronous programming with async views and middleware, enabling developers to handle long-running tasks, I/O-bound operations, and high-concurrency scenarios efficiently.

13. Deployment:

1. **Definition**: Deployment is the process of making a web application available for public access, typically on a production server or hosting platform.
2. **Usage**: Django applications can be deployed to various hosting environments, including traditional servers, cloud platforms, and containerization platforms, using deployment tools and techniques.

14. Scalability:

1. **Definition**: Scalability refers to the ability of a web application to handle increasing levels of traffic, users, and data volume without sacrificing performance or reliability.

2. **Usage**: Django applications can be scaled horizontally or vertically using techniques such as load balancing, caching, database optimization, and distributed architecture.

15. Security:

1. **Definition**: Security is paramount in web development, encompassing measures to protect web applications from threats such as unauthorized access, data breaches, injection attacks, and cross-site scripting (XSS).
2. **Usage**: Django incorporates security features such as built-in protections against common vulnerabilities, secure authentication mechanisms, input validation, and encryption to ensure robust security posture in web applications.

Summary: This glossary provides a comprehensive overview of key web development terms relevant to Django full stack development. Understanding these terms is essential for Django developers to communicate effectively, navigate the development process, and build secure,

www.ingramcontent.com/pod-product-compliance
Lightning Source LLC
Chambersburg PA
CBHW031235050326
40690CB00007B/808